YORK NOT

General Editors: Professo
of Stirling) & Professor S
University of Beirut)

Thomas Middleton and William Rowley

THE CHANGELING

Notes by Neil King

BA (DURHAM) PGCE (CAMBRIDGE)
Senior Master and Head of English, Hymers College, Hull

LONGMAN
YORK PRESS

To the memory of my Father and Mother

The illustration of the Globe Playhouse is from *The Globe Restored in Theatre: A Way of Seeing* by C. Walter Hodges, published by Oxford University Press. ©Oxford University Press

YORK PRESS
Immeuble Esseily, Place Riad Solh, Beirut.

LONGMAN GROUP UK LIMITED
Longman House,
Burnt Mill,
Harlow,
Essex.

First published 1983
Second impression 1986

ISBN 0-582-79238-X

Produced by Longman Group (FE) Ltd
Printed in Hong Kong

Contents

Contents

Part 1

Introduction

Thomas Middleton (1580–1625)

Thomas Middleton was born in London, the son of William Middleton, citizen and bricklayer, a man who was one of the prosperous commercial middle class. In 1586 William Middleton died, leaving a reasonable inheritance to his wife, Anne, and his two children. However, later in the same year Anne married Thomas Harvey, a penniless adventurer, and there followed a series of intrigues and lawsuits to protect her first husband's legacy. In 1590 Harvey went off on adventures in the Low Countries and Portugal, but returned to pester the family. On one occasion his stepson had to evict him from the family home. In 1598 Thomas Middleton went up to Queen's College, Oxford, but lack of money, probably the result of the litigation against Harvey, meant that he found it difficult to support himself, and there is no evidence that he ever took a degree.

Before 1600 he wrote poems, none of them very good; by that date he was settled in London and working with acting companies. By 1604 he was married, had a son, and was writing comedies for Philip Henslowe (?–1616) and other theatre managers. Over the next twenty years he wrote or collaborated in the writing of many plays. To begin with he wrote mainly comedies, although it is now thought by various critics that he was the author of *The Revenger's Tragedy* (?1607), which is traditionally ascribed to Cyril Tourneur (?1575–1626). His comedies portray cunning tradesmen, con-men, courtesans, gallants, rich widows and the like, and his ironic views of the commercial and sexual activities of London citizens resemble those of the satiric comedies of Ben Jonson (1573–1637). The best of them are *The Roaring Girl* (?1610), written with Thomas Dekker (?1572–?1632), *A Trick to Catch the Old One* (?1606), *Michaelmas Term* (?1606), *A Mad World, My Masters* (?1606), *A Chaste Maid in Cheapside* (?1612); and a number of others written in collaboration with William Rowley (?1585–?1637). Middleton also collaborated from time to time with Michael Drayton (1563–1631), Frances Beaumont (?1584–1616), Anthony Munday (?1553–1633) and John Webster (?1580–?1625) on plays now lost. *A Fair Quarrel* (?1616), another play written in conjunction with William Rowley, has the ethics of fighting duels for 'honour' as its main theme, and is best described as a tragi-comedy. With *Women Beware Women* (?1621) and *The Changeling* (1622) came his notable tragedies. The latter, again written with Rowley, is perhaps his masterpiece; and it has proved consistently popular with audiences from its first production. *A Game at Chess*, a satire directed against King James I's (1566–1625) alliance with Spain, was performed by the King's Men, the company to which William Shakespeare had belonged, in 1624. The attack on Spain was popular but brought official disapproval; members of the King's Men were imprisoned for a short time, and Middleton had to go into hiding. The trouble blew over, but after this he wrote no more plays.

A comprehensive list of his works may be found in the Introduction to *The Selected Plays of Thomas Middleton*, edited by David L. Frost for the Plays by Renaissance and Restoration Dramatists series, Cambridge University Press, Cambridge, 1978, pp. xiv-xvi.

William Rowley (?1585–?1637)

Very little is known about the life of William Rowley. He was probably born in London. By 1610 he was an actor with the company of the Duke of York's Men, which was later to become Prince Charles's Men. He joined the King's Men in about 1623. In 1609 he had published *A Search for Money*, a pamphlet on certain literary fashions of the time which gives a lively picture of contemporary London life. He met Thomas Middleton in about 1614, but he had begun writing plays before then. Few of the fifty plays in which he is known to have had a hand now exist. His best solo effort is *All's Lost by Lust* (?1619), part romantic comedy, part morality play, which is characterised by crude but powerful dramatic verse. Other extant plays include *A New Wonder, A Woman Never Vext* (?1610) and *A Match at Mid-Night* (?1622). He collaborated with Middleton on *The Old Law* (?1615), in which Massinger also had a hand, *Wit at Several Weapons* (?1616) and *The World Tost at Tennis* (1620), and on *A Fair Quarrel* and *The Changeling*. In both of these last two Rowley was principally responsible for the subplot and helped with the overall planning. Apart from the above-mentioned plays, the best one in which he had a hand was *The Witch of Edmonton* (1621), of which Thomas Dekker and John Ford (1586–?1639) were co-authors. A powerful revival of this play was produced by the Royal Shakespeare Company in 1981.

English drama 1560–1642

The whole of this period of drama is sometimes referred to as 'Elizabethan Drama', and not unreasonably so, as the play-writing of the period gained its initial momentum under Elizabeth, and, although the tone of the plays changed during the early years of the seventeenth century, the era as a whole represents the first and greatest age of English drama. Strictly speaking, Elizabethan Drama ends with the death of Queen Elizabeth I in 1603, and after the accession of James I in that year we should talk of Jacobean Drama. When James I was succeeded by his son, Charles I, in 1625, the period known as Caroline Drama begins: but this is a term that is rarely used.

Elizabethan drama

In about 1561 a play called *Gorboduc* was produced. It was significant in a number of ways: it was the first play in England that can be properly called a full-length play; it was the first English tragedy, although it adhered closely to the style of the Latin tragic playwright Seneca (4 BC–AD 65); it was the first play to base its story on chronicles of English history; and it was the first play to be written in blank verse. The authors were Thomas Norton (1532–84) and Thomas Sackville (1532–1608), both notable politicians and well-educated men, and their play marked the beginning of drama as an increasingly popular form of literature. Travelling companies of actors had certainly for some time provided welcome entertainment in tavern courtyards and manor houses up and down the country; but now plays were becoming fashionable at the Universities of Oxford and Cambridge, the two major seats of learning, and also at court where *Gorboduc* was presented before the Queen in 1562, the first of a considerable list of performances recorded as acted before her; and her liking for dramatic performance must have influenced the taste of her court.

Stage plays seem to have suited the out-going exuberance of the Elizabethans, with their love of both the refined and the earthy, their ability to enjoy a sublime madrigal and a scurrilous, obscene ballad. Many of the plays were crude in structure and written in bombastic language – a typical example is *The Life of Cambises, King of Persia*, written in the early years of Elizabeth's reign some time before 1570. The author may have been Thomas Preston (dates unknown). The overblown style of *Cambises* became proverbial, still being good for a joke over twenty years later in William Shakespeare's (1564–1616) *Henry IV, Part One* (?1597). A more refined play was *Supposes* (1566) by George Gascoigne (?1542–78): this comedy was very successful in its time, anticipating the plays of the University Wits.

This is a name given to a group of men, all educated at either Oxford or Cambridge, who wrote plays for performance at their respective universities, and who later worked in London during the second half of Elizabeth's reign. John Lyly (?1554–1606) wrote *Endymion* (1588) and other courtly plays which did much to shape and give discipline to dramatic styles. He is best known, not for a play, but for his book *Euphues* (1579). This was written in a very artificial style, full of elaborate elegancies, and for some years set a fashion for writing and even speaking; but by the 1590s there had been a move towards a more terse, direct style. Thomas Nashe (1567–1601), Thomas Lodge (?1558–1625) and George Peele (?1558–?97) – renowned for his dissipated way of living – were all playwrights of note in the circle of University Wits, but the member of the group who achieved more than any other was Christopher Marlowe (1564–93).

Marlowe is indisputably the best Elizabethan dramatist before Shakespeare. A declared atheist and a controversial figure in other ways, his major contribution to the field of drama is twofold. Firstly, he managed to breathe more life into his characters, making them more memorable by developing the rather stiff and academic structure of the plays of his time and creating greater flexibility within the accepted dramatic form. He frequently pulled the action of a play together under the influence of one dominant character, as in *Tamburlaine* (1587), *Doctor Faustus* (1588) and *The Jew of Malta* (1589), giving to the action a unity of purpose which had been rare in earlier plays. Marlowe's second great contribution to drama owes much to the fact that he was essentially a poet who had turned his attention to the stage; consequently he possessed the skill not merely to adopt the rather wooden and contrived blank verse, which, since *Gorboduc*, had become the accepted metre of dramatic writing, but to shape and develop it into a powerful and fitting vehicle for his dramatic language. Years later Ben Jonson, one of the best playwrights of the Jacobean Age, was to pay tribute to what he called 'Marlowe's mighty line'. Undoubtedly a potentially great English dramatist was lost when Marlowe was stabbed to death in a Deptford tavern, apparently as the result of an argument over a bill for supper and ale.

Robert Greene (?1560–92) was a typical member of the University Wits. He wrote prolifically, his output including a variety of plays, works of prose romance, and many pamphlets – of which the most entertaining for the modern reader are his 'coney-catching' pamphlets, a series of essays warning against the ways of the Elizabethan underworld and cataloguing the various types of criminal. In one pamphlet, *A Groatsworth of Wit* (1592), written in a state of bitterness and poverty at the end of his life, he seems to be warning his fellow University men against an uneducated fellow, 'an upstart crow, beautified with our feathers, that . . . supposes he is as well able to bombast out a blank verse as the best of you; and . . . is in his own conceit the only Shake-scene in a country' with his 'tiger's heart wrapped in a player's hide'. This can only be a reference to William Shakespeare, an actor who had apparently decided that he could write plays as good as those in which he was currently acting.

Although Shakespeare was already in London and writing plays before Marlowe's death, his mature period of writing probably began around the year 1593, and it seems almost as if his early years were an apprenticeship, taking up Marlowe's role and continuing the development and refinement of dramatic structure, characterisation and verse which Marlowe had begun. We cannot be sure of the dates of most of Shakespeare's plays because frequently we do not know when they received their first public performances, and there seemed to be no hurry to publish them. This was probably because Shakespeare and his contemporaries felt that plays were essentially matter to be acted, seen and heard rather than printed and read. Also, the printing of a play could be dangerous: no laws of copyright existed, and printing would have made easy the pirating and performing of a play by a rival company. We have, however, an idea of the chronological order in which Shakespeare's plays were written, and even the 'apprenticeship pieces' of the very late 1580s and early 1590s can in retrospect be seen to be among the best of their time. He experimented with the Roman-style Plautine comedy in, for example, *The Comedy of Errors* (?1589), with the Roman-style Senecan revenge tragedy in, for example, *Titus Andronicus* (?1592), with the by now traditional chronicle play in, for example, the three parts of *Henry VI* (?1590–1592). With *Richard III* (?1593) he made his contribution to the ranks of Machiavellian megalomaniac monsters so much enjoyed by theatre-going Elizabethans. As his confidence and his control of his medium grew in the 1590s, he wrote better-balanced history plays, for example, *Richard II* (1595) and the two parts of *Henry IV* (1597–8), which were much more sophisticated than the older Elizabethan chronicle plays. He wrote *Love's Labour's Lost* (?1593) which, although some critics believe this to be one of his earliest plays, is startlingly inventive in its exciting use of language, and must have seemed very bright and original when first performed; and he wrote a series of exuberant comedies, for example, *Much Ado About Nothing* (?1598) and *As You Like It* (?1599), much of the plot of which he took from *Rosalynde* (1590), a prose romance by Thomas Lodge, who had himself taken the story from an earlier source. The creation of an original story by a writer was not considered necessary at this time: a prose piece or play was judged by how well a story, if it was well known, was developed and enhanced. Another prose romance, Robert Greene's *Pandosto* (1588), was later to be taken by Shakespeare and used as a source for part of *The Winter's Tale* (?1611); if Greene had still been alive he would doubtless have seen this as a bitter irony in view of his warning of some seventeen years before. With *Romeo and Juliet* (?1596) came Shakespeare's first well-known tragedy. The tragic elements in the play are largely derived from the fact that the lovers are 'star-crossed', and the play does not have the power of Shakespeare's Jacobean tragedies, which tend to grow out of deep flaws and inconsistencies inside the nature of man himself, for example *King Lear* (?1606). By the time Shakespeare had come to write *Twelfth Night* (?1600) even his comedies have their dark side which looks forward to the less assured spirit of the Jacobean Age.

Jacobean drama

There is a noticeable change in the tone of plays written during the early years of James's reign, even by dramatists such as Shakespeare and Jonson who were writing during the reigns of both Elizabeth and James.

Although a man of wide interests and a patron of the arts, King James was not an attractive figure to many of his subjects. Religious discontent was rife: the Puritan movement, out of sympathy with most entertainments and condemning playhouses as dens of vice, was gaining in strength; and ferment amongst the Catholic population was epitomised by the Gunpowder Plot of 1605, when a group of Catholics plotted to blow up the King and his entire parliament. Scientific discovery was accelerating at a great pace, and for the first time men of learning began to realise that it was not possible to know everything that was worth knowing. Sir Francis Bacon (1561–1626) is one of the last representatives of a breed of men whose competence embraced literature and the arts, philosophy and science. In the same way that the general confidence of nineteenth-century Victorian Britain that all things were possible has been replaced by the uncertainty and self-consciousness of the twentieth century, so the Jacobean of, say, 1610 may well have looked back with nostalgia on the closing decades of the previous century; the reign of Elizabeth may have appeared to him as halcyon days, crowned by Sir Francis Drake's (?1540–96) defeat of the Spanish Armada in 1588. Despite the fact that the last two decades of Elizabeth's reign had their troubles, the drama of the period had been, generally speaking, firm and assured: the tragedies were often bold portraits of villains who were defeated by the forces of good in the end; the histories usually ended with consoling affirmations that a moral order and a God-ordained hierarchical society existed; and the comedies and pastoral romances were in the main sunny and carefree.

The drama of the Jacobean Age was altogether more sombre. The tragedies now tended to explore corrupt worlds where human nature was rotten, and evil was not the product of a single grand villain whose expunging offered the possibility of a speedy return to a better society. The creations of playwrights such as George Chapman (?1559–1634), Cyril Tourneur, Thomas Middleton, John Webster and the Jacobean

Shakespeare are ambiguous; and the source of the corruption of their characters was often specifically sexual. The comedies of the period are rarely pastoral romances. The elegiac notes of Shakespeare's *Twelfth Night* have given way to the uncertain discords of his *Measure for Measure* (?1604). To list as a comedy his *Troilus and Cressida* (?1602) where only wars and lechery hold fashion and where a lusty boy turns into a cynic baying for bloody revenge, is indeed a sick joke. Shakespeare must have been very depressed about mankind when he wrote that play. So-called 'citizen' comedies became popular, for example, Middleton's *A Chaste Maid in Cheapside*, which satirised the behaviour of middle-class town-dwellers. Ben Johnson's *Bartholomew Fair* (1614) and his *The Alchemist* (1612) are panoplies of London's teeming life; although vivid, they display the full range of human rapacity, material and sexual. Two of the harshest and most unpleasant satires on greed are Jonson's *Volpone* (1606) and John Marston's (?1576–1634) tragi-comedy *The Malcontent* (1604).

The pleasure-loving court of the permissive King James began to voice its growing demand for elaborate masques and spectacles, and the emphasis on words and their poetic effect within drama began to wane. The quality of plays diminished in the 1620s, yet out of their decadence flared the occasional powerful drama such as *'Tis Pity She's a Whore* (?1627) by John Ford (1586–?1640). Nothing memorable was written during the 1630s, and by 1642 the public theatres were shut down.

The playhouses

Before the Elizabethan Age plays were performed in a variety of places: biblical plays (called Miracle plays) were staged in churchyards or market squares; there were performances of plays dealing with various Vices and Virtues (Morality plays) in open-air arenas; occasionally, small professional touring companies would visit a town and be allowed to put on a play in an inn courtyard – and, if they were lucky, they might be invited to the local manor house or castle to perform an 'interlude' for the diversion of the local gentry: and rather academic comedies and tragedies, usually derived from the classical world, were performed in schools and universities. But there was no such thing as a theatre.

In 1575 James Burbage, father of the great Shakespearean actor Richard Burbage, built in Finsbury fields to the north of the City of London the first building in England since Roman times that was specifically intended for theatrical performance. He called it, appropriately enough, 'The Theatre'. During the following decades several more open-air playhouses were built around London. The city authorities would not allow them to be built within the city, deeming them places of riot and breeding grounds for vice (theatre people themselves have never been considered quite respectable): so the theatres were sited in the fields to the north and west of the city, or behind the 'stews' (brothels) on the south bank of the Thames. These playhouses fostered a truly popular drama, and people from all strata of society, from apprentices to gallants, crowded into their yards and galleries, and even sat upon the stage itself – up to two thousand attending a single performance in some cases.

In 1599 the lease ran out on the ground upon which The Theatre stood, and the landlord refused to renew it; perhaps he hoped to cash in easily on the increasingly lucrative theatre business by capturing a playhouse when the Lord Chamberlain's Men, now headed by Richard Burbage, were forced to abandon it. If, so, he was to be disappointed. Virtually overnight, the company dismantled the playhouse, carted the timbers across the river, re-erected it on the south bank, and re-named it 'The Globe' (see illustration opposite). This is the theatre in which many of Shakespeare's plays were first performed. The company (re-named 'The King's Men' after King James I's accession) also owned an indoor theatre at Blackfriars: this drew a more select audience. From time to time they were invited to perform at court.

There are two excellent short books which give an introduction to the playhouses of the period. They are:

JIM BRADBURY: *Shakespeare and his Theatre*, Longman, London, 1975.

C. WALTER HODGES: *Shakespeare's Theatre*, Oxford University Press, Oxford, 1964.

A good idea of the probable nature of the audiences is given in:

ALFRED HARBAGE: *Shakespeare's Audience*, Columbia University Press, New York and London, 1941.

A note on the text

The principal source for the main plot of *The Changeling* is the fourth story in Book One of *The Triumphs of God's Revenge against the Crying and Execrable Sin of Wilful and Premeditated Murder*, a collection of stories by John Reynolds (dates unknown) which was published in 1621. An examination of this source will show how skilfully Middleton and Rowley adapted their raw material for the stage. Another source is a translation of a Spanish story by Leonard Digges (dates unknown), which he called *Gerardo, the Unfortunate Spaniard* (1622).

A licence was granted on 7 May 1622 for performance of *The Changeling* by the Lady Elizabeth's Servants at the Phoenix, and it seems that the play was immediately popular. There are records of performances at Whitehall on Sunday, 4 January 1623/4, in March 1634/5, and sometime during or after 1639. However, the play was not printed, so far as we know, until the quarto edition of 1653, the title page

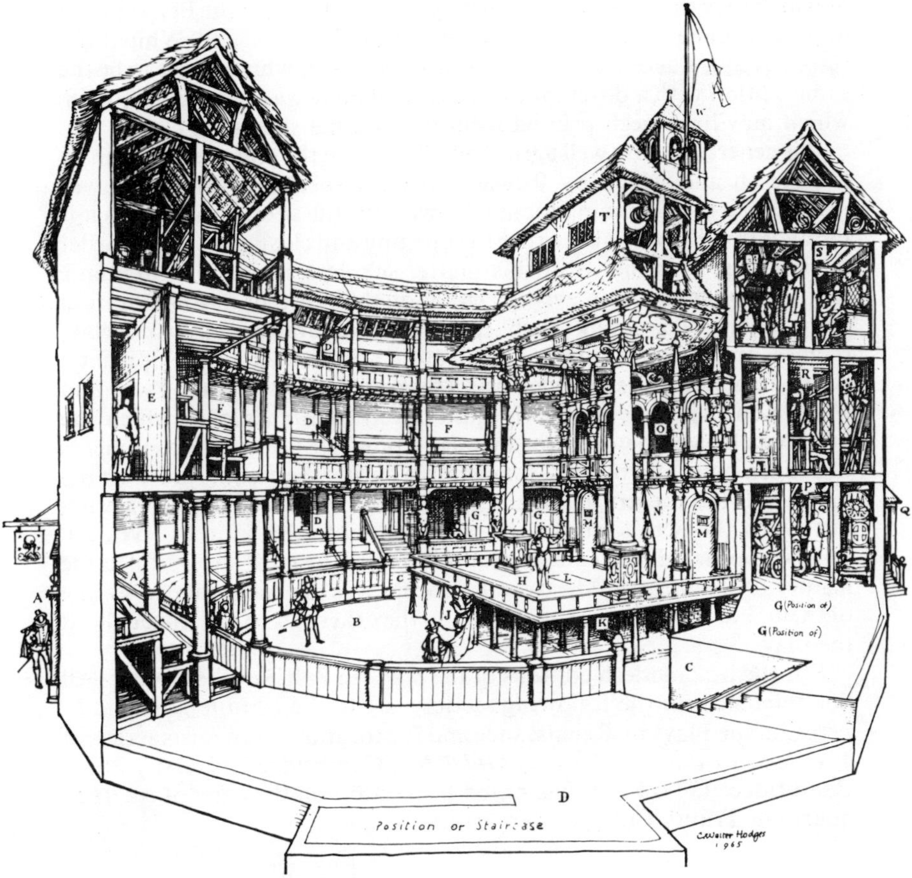

A CONJECTURAL RECONSTRUCTION OF THE INTERIOR OF THE GLOBE PLAYHOUSE

AA Main entrance
B The Yard
CC Entrances to lowest gallery
D Entrance to staircase and upper galleries
E Corridor serving the different sections of the middle gallery
F Middle gallery ('Twopenny Rooms')
G 'Gentlemen's Rooms' or Lords' Rooms'
H The stage
J The hanging being put up round the stage
K The 'Hell' under the stage
L The stage trap, leading down to the Hell
MM Stage doors
N Curtained 'place behind the stage'
O Gallery above the stage, used as required sometimes by musicians, sometimes by spectators, and often as part of the play
P Back-stage area (the tiring-house)
Q Tiring-house door
R Dressing-rooms
S Wardrobe and storage
T The hut housing the machine for lowering enthroned gods, etc., to the stage
U The 'Heavens'
W Hoisting the playhouse flag

of which says that it was 'acted (with great Applause) at the Privat house in Drury Lane and Salisbury Court' (the Phoenix and Whitefriars respectively). There was another printing in 1653, which seems to be the same edition with a different title page; and there was an edition in 1668, which may have been printed from the original sheets.

It is generally fairly well agreed which parts of the play were written by Middleton and which by Rowley. Broadly speaking, Middleton was responsible for the main plot and Rowley for the subplot, although it is thought that Rowley also wrote the opening and closing scenes. In order to make up their minds in this matter scholars study other dramatic writings by the two men, written either on their own or in collaboration with others, examining such features as characteristic word-play, themes, images, vocabulary, versification and character development.* As an actor-dramatist Rowley was a thorough theatre man in a way that Middleton was not, and it is quite likely that in scenes which are otherwise by Middleton, Rowley was responsible for handling moments of sudden noise and bustle – for example during the commotion over the fire in V.1. His theatrical instinct would have been invaluable in sensing just when the action needed to be moved onto this kind of level. All things considered, the collaboration is one of the most successful in the history of the theatre. The overall concept was probably shaped by one of them, but the influence of each upon the other can be seen throughout the play.

For the best modern editions of the play see Part 5 of these notes. All line references in the following sections are to the edition by David L. Frost, in the Plays by Renaissance and Restoration Dramatists series, of *The Selected Plays of Thomas Middleton*, Cambridge University Press, Cambridge, 1978. Frost has based his edition on the copy of the 1653 quarto at Trinity College, Cambridge.

*For a full consideration of this see the introduction to N.W. Bawcutt's Revels edition of the play, Methuen, London, 1958, pp. xxxix-xliv.

Part 2

Summaries
of THE CHANGELING

A general summary

The play is set in Alicante, Spain. Alsemero, an inveterate traveller, has fallen in love with Beatrice-Joanna, and to the amazement of his friend Jasperino is disinclined to sail on to Malta. Jasperino decides to amuse himself by attempting to seduce Diaphanta, Beatrice's waiting-woman. It turns out that Alsemero's father was an old friend of Beatrice's father, Vermandero, who invites Alsemero to stay at his castle. Beatrice returns Alsemero's love, but the bar to any further thoughts of marriage is that Beatrice has recently become betrothed to one Alonzo de Piracquo, and Vermandero is set upon the match. The wedding is to take place in one week's time.

At a nearby madhouse Alibius, the doctor in charge, is frightened that his young wife will be seduced by gallants who occasionally visit the mad folk. He tells his assistant, Lollio, to keep a close eye on her. Antonio, an idiot, is admitted to the asylum.

The scene moves to the castle where Beatrice tries to delay her marriage to Alonzo. Tomazo, Alonzo's brother, notices that Beatrice does not seem overjoyed at the prospect of her marriage, and is quick to see that the most likely reason is that she loves someone else. Alonzo rejects his brother's misgivings. Beatrice and Alsemero meet secretly. Alsemero suggest that he should challenge Alonzo to a fight over her, but she sees that if he were to kill Alonzo then he would be condemned by the law and they would be no better off. She suddenly thinks of De Flores, a follower of her father for whom she has shown a hatred which is quite irrational beyond the mere fact that the man has an ugly face. She resolves to use him in order to dispose of Alonzo de Piracquo, thinking that she 'shall rid myself/Of two inveterate loathings at one time' (II.2.144–5). When De Flores appears, she plays upon his interest in her to induce him to murder Alonzo for reward. He agrees with alacrity. She believes that the reward he desires is money, not realising that the reward he intends to claim is her body, after which he has long lusted. He has observed the meeting between Beatrice and Alsemero, and considers that Beatrice is potentially promiscuous.

An opportunity to carry out the assassination presents itself almost immediately when Alonzo asks De Flores to show him round the castle's fortifications. In an obscure part of the castle, De Flores kills him and hides the body.

In the madhouse, Isabella, Alibius's young wife, is chafing under the restraint of not being allowed out and about. She agrees to let Lollio show her 'the pleasure of your bedlam' (III.3.24). First Franciscus is brought in; he is apparently a mad poet who has lost his wits over the love of a chambermaid. Then Antonio, the recently committed fool, is allowed in. While Lollio is out of the room, Antonio reveals to Isabella that he is quite sane and has had himself committed in order to gain access to her. She rejects his advances. Lollio spies on what is going on, and warns Isabella that if she gives in to Antonio then he (Lollio) will expect his share of sexual pleasure with her.

Back at the castle, De Flores returns to Beatrice to announce that Alonzo is dead and to claim his reward. She is aghast to find that it is not money but her virginity that he wants, and realises too late that murder leads to other sins. Everyone else is perplexed at Alonzo's disappearance. Vermandero decides, to general approval, that Alsemero shall fill Alonzo's place and marry Beatrice, who by now has been deflowered by De Flores, and is terrified that on her wedding night Alsemero will realise that she is not *virgo intacta*. She discovers a private closet used by Alsemero, opens it, and finds inside various medicines and drugs, including a potion which is supposed to determine whether or not a women is a maid. She tries out the potion on Diaphanta, who yawns, sneezes, laughs and then becomes melancholy, just as the instructions with the potion say a true maid will do. Professing fear at losing her virginity, Beatrice easily bribes the libidinous Diaphanta to replace her in the darkness of the bridal bed, agreeing that they should exchange places again at midnight.

Tomazo is convinced that his brother has been done away with, and is desperately trying to find out who is responsible. He rages at Vermandero, and accuses Alsemero of foul play. Alsemero is further disturbed on his wedding day by news that Beatrice has been observed having a secret meeting with De Flores, whom he knows she loathes. He makes Beatrice undergo the virginity test, and she is able to simulate the symptoms which she observed in Diaphanta, and thus satisfy Alsemero as to her purity.

Meanwhile, at the madhouse, Isabella shows Lollio a love letter she has received from Franciscus who, it turns out, is also pretending. She and Lollio decide to have some fun at the expense of these 'counterfeit madmen', leading on Antonio and Franciscus, truly making fools of them, and persuading them that each can only win the love of Isabella by eliminating the other from the reckoning.

In the castle, affairs are coming to a head for Beatrice. It is past midnight of the wedding night, and the lustful Diaphanta has failed to leave Alsemero's bed. De Flores enters, and Beatrice despairs as the clock strikes two, then three, and discovery comes closer. Alonzo's ghost appears, the second time it has come to De Flores. De Flores devises a plan. He starts a fire in Diaphanta's chamber, rouses the house, and them kills Diaphanta when she returns to her room. In the confusion, Beatrice manages to take her place beside Alsemero. De Flores is praised all round for his handling of the fire, and Beatrice encourages the others to reward him. De Flores now admires her cunning as much as she admires his.

Tomazo has begun to feel that 'honest De Flores' may not be so honest after all. De Flores fears the instinct of the brother of the man he has murdered, and tries to steer clear of him. However, Vermandero tells Tomazo that two men have been arrested who disappeared at just the time of the murder. They are Antonio and Franciscus, discovered in the local madhouse.

Beatrice is again seen leaving a secret meeting with De Flores. Alsemero confronts her. She admits murder for his sake, but denies adultery. He locks her in his closet, then confronts De Flores, who cheerfully admits all, adding that Beatrice is a whore. She screams her denial from the closet. Alsemero locks De Flores in with her, and tells Vermandero that he knows who the real murderers are. He then lets the guilty pair out of the closet but finds that De Flores has stabbed Beatrice. Before she dies she confesses everything. De Flores stabs himself and also dies. The moral of the play is made clear: justice has been done. Tomazo is satisfied. Alsemero comments on all the people in the play who are, in one way or another, changelings. He offers 'a son's duty' to Vermandero and, in an epilogue, asks the audience for their approval.

Detailed summaries

Act I Scene I

The opening scene is clearly intended to be set outside or near a church. Alsemero is saying, in a soliloquy, that he first saw the woman he loves in church, and he looks forward to making their relationship perfect by marrying her there. Jasperino, his friend, enters, reporting that the wind is set fair for their voyage to Malta; but he finds Alsemero unusually disinclined to travel abroad. His servants are all ready to load his trunks on board ship, but he stops them. Jasperino comments that Alsemero has never been susceptible to love, so it cannot be that which holds him ashore; and then, the next moment, he marvels to see Alsemero greet and kiss a woman who has entered with her waiting-woman and servants. Alsemero declares his love for this woman, whose name is

Beatrice; and it has clearly been a case of love at first sight, for she warns him against judging by appearances. Alsemero protests that his eyes and judgment both agree, and he only waits for her agreement. Aside, Beatrice says that this is the man for her, but implies that she has plighted her troth to someone else only five days before.

Jasperino decides to make advances to Diaphanta, Beatrice's waiting-woman. De Flores appears, a gentleman who is a follower of Vermandero, Beatrice's father. He announces that Vermandero is coming, but for his trouble he is spoken to scornfully by Beatrice. She tells Alsemero that she cannot stand the sight of the man, although she is unable to give good reason why. De Flores is well aware of her aversion to him, but is determined to enjoy looking at her when he can. Alsemero says that every person has an unreasonable dislike of something, no matter how normal he is in most respects: he himself cannot endure cherries. Meanwhile, Jasperino's wooing of Diaphanta has already reached the stage of exchanging sexual innuendos.

Vermandero enters, having come to meet Beatrice as she returns from church. Beatrice introduces Alsemero to her father, and it emerges that he is the son of an old friend and comrade-in-arms of Vermandero, who invites him to his castle. All seems to be going as Alsemero could wish until he hears that Beatrice is to marry one Piracquo in seven days' time. Beatrice protests to her father that she needs more time to be reconciled to the loss of her virginity. As they leave, Beatrice drops a glove which De Flores, at Vermandero's bidding, picks up. Beatrice furiously throws down the other glove, saying that she will not wear one that De Flores has touched.

Left alone, De Flores says that, despite her treatment of him, he loves her, and declares darkly: 'if but to vex her, I'll haunt her still;/Though I get nothing else, I'll have my will' (I.1.237–8).

NOTES AND GLOSSARY:

Beatrice-Joanna: there is no clear reason why Beatrice-Joanna is given two names. One explanation could be that the playwrights wish to indicate two sides to her character. It may be significant that her father alone calls her Joanna, perhaps indicating the good side of her character.

None but imaginary: no omen except one created in the imagination

holy purpose: marriage

the place blest: the Garden of Eden, man's first home

hath first begun our: witnessed our first

buy a gale amongst the witches: a popular superstition had it that witches controlled the winds. Compare Shakespeare, *Macbeth*, I.3.11

pennyworth: bargain

a' God's name: free, gratis
Even now: just now
vane: weather vane
doubt: fear
trap your horses for the speed: harness the horses yourself in order to speed up the departure
weigh the anchor with 'em: help the crew to haul up the anchor
foremost breath: first breath of wind
orisons: prayers
stoic: here, a man free from passion
found: confirmed
beauty: beautiful women
of/Somewhat: upon something
a-going: preparing to go
board: take on board ship
Aquarius: Aquarius is the eleventh sign of the Zodiac, and means the 'Water-carrier'. Hence, Jasperino is saying that this is a 'critical' or most favourable time for a sea-voyage
this smoke will bring forth fire: from the proverb 'there's no smoke without fire', that is 'there's something the matter here'
Ere: before
your pleasure: we will do as it pleases you
The laws of the Medes: unchangeable laws (see the Bible, Daniel 6:8)
in my conscience: upon my word, indeed
ransom'd . . . from the Turk: Greece was at this time under Turkish rule
sing at first sight: (1) sight-read music, (2) make love at first sight (compare Shakespeare, *Troilus and Cressida*, V.2.9)
want: lack
Our eyes are sentinels . . .: this speech expresses a commonplace in Elizabethan literature; namely, that seeing with the eye does not necessarily mean seeing (that is, understanding) with the mind. Compare Shakespeare, *King Lear*, where the metaphor runs throughout the play
further: past that point
Both Houses then consenting . . .: both Houses of Parliament, the Lords and the Commons (that is, the senses and the judgment) having approved, the bill only needs the Queen's signature (that is, Beatrice's consent) to make it law (that is, a firm pledging of their mutual love)
one above me: her father

carriers: land transport
at farthest: (1) as far as we are likely to go in our journey, (2) quite off course
sure: indeed, certainly
Methinks: I think
lawful prize: a vessel which no regulations prohibit him from capturing
down goes her topsail: the sign of a ship's surrender. This kind of nautical imagery in connection with the wooing of a woman is frequent in the literature of the period.
stall/A good presence: forestall the welcome appearance (of her father)
Will't never mend . . . other?: will she never cease to scorn me, or I to expose myself to her scorn?
enjoin'd: commanded (by my lust)
If but to spite: if only in despite of
his or hers: anyone else's reason
basilisk: a mythical reptile hatched by a serpent from a cock's egg; its breath, even its look, was fatal
distastes: dislikes
infinites: innumerable people
countenance: face
My memory has: I can remember
In good respect with: well thought of by
follows him: is one of his retainers
I am a mad wag, wench . . . . another time I'll show thee all: George Williams, in the introduction to his edition of the play, comments upon this exchange (I.1.137–53) as follows: 'Jasperino professes himself a physician and prescribes for his madness the cure of love. Diaphanta directs him to Alibius, the only genuine doctor in the play. This interchange serves many functions. It delineates the character of Diaphanta as unashamedly lustful and thus prepares for the misadventures of V.1. It serves as a coarse foil to the polite love-making of Alsemero and Beatrice and thus associates the immodesty of Diaphanta with the "modesty" of Beatrice. It unites the metaphor of sickness to the concept of madness and suggests that the madness of lovers is not far from the madness of madmen. It advances two herbs as medicatives, the poppy and the cuckoo. Both of them have erotic connotations, but the cuckoo is as well a remedy for diseases of the brain' (*The Changeling*, ed. George Williams, Arnold, London, 1967, p.xxi)

simple: medicinal herb
cuckoo: wild arum or cuckoo-pint, which is of phallic shape
change my saint: saint here means the object of my adoration
beholding: indebted
an article between: one condition
promonts': promontories'
native: local to the area, Alicante being about seventy-five miles south of Valencia
To call me so: 'my best love'
were worth Iulan down: had shown the first growth of hair. Iulus Ascanius was the adolescent son of Aeneas (by his wife Creusa, daughter of Priam King of Troy) in Virgil's (70–19BC) epic poem the *Aeneid*
went together: were his equal
Saint Jacques: the patron saint of Spain
came behind: was not as good as
Swallowed him: saw his death (the metaphor suggests that he died by drowning)
the late league: a reference to an actual twelve-year truce between Spain and Holland, which expired in 1621. This allusion helps to confirm the date of the play
'twas time to breathe: it was a welcome interval in Spain's wars
ha': have
toy: trifling thing
think myself unkindly us'd: be offended
occasions: affairs, business
Bound . . . bound: indebted . . . united. A punning use of both senses of the word
want/My will: lack what I desire
by the way: as we walk along
murderers: small cannons
t'other's: the other's
'em: them
favour: token of love
mischief: ill wish
thrust my fingers . . .: there is deliberate sexual suggestiveness here

Act I Scene 2

The second scene is set in a madhouse. Alibius, the doctor in charge, is confiding to Lollio, his assistant, that he is frightened of being cuckolded by his wife, who is much younger than he is. He instructs Lollio to keep a close eye on her. He is particularly concerned that those who occasionally come to visit the mad folk do not see his wife.

Alibius has been expecting a new madman to be admitted to the asylum. He duly arrives, brought by a gentleman called Pedro, who gives money to Alibius and Lollio, urging them to take good care of the madman, whose name is Antonio. Lollio promises that he will 'bring him up to my own pitch . . . make him as wise as myself' (I.2.137–8). Pedro leaves, and at first Antonio is distressed. Lollio pacifies him, and then proceeds to ask him questions in order to decide in which form to place him. To begin with Antonio answers well, but the questions become more difficult as Lollio begins to indulge in witty obscurities. The test is interrupted by a clamour of madmen, and Alibius notes that it is time to feed them. As he leaves, he reminds Lollio of his 'last charge', presumably referring to his wife. Lollio leads off Antonio to join the other madmen.

NOTES AND GLOSSARY:

Antonio: although Antonio, who appears for the first time in this scene, is called 'the Changeling', it does not follow that he is the most important character in the play. The play is called *The Changeling* for many reasons, and an assessment of the significance of the titles is to be found on pp. 84–6 in Part 4 of these Notes

close to: discreet with

allow: grant, admit

go about: am talking about

meet'st the substance of the point: put your finger on the problem

Shrewd application: astute thinking

ring: with an allusion to the female pudendum

finger: with the secondary meaning of 'penis'

thrusting into't: compare I.1.234

conceiv'st me: understand what I am talking about

look out: (1) travel away from home, (2) beware

comfortable: comforting

daily visitants: Bethlehem Hospital (Bedlam) in London and other lunatic asylums were visited as places of entertainment, in much the same way as nowadays people go to see animals in a zoo

habits: dress, clothes

shrewd: serious

serve the turn: (1) show them round, (2) that is, you are a fool and I am mad

ward: guard (a fencing position)

buckler: shield

pluck a rose: with a secondary meaning of 'urinate'

***like an idiot*:** this probably means, apart from his behaviour, that Antonio would be wearing a long-skirted coat and high, conical hat (the traditional 'dunce's' cap), and dangling an elementary school book from his wrist
speaks itself: speaks for itself
takes off the labour of my tongue: removes the need for me to explain
pains: trouble
commodious: medically effective
patterns: samples
sweet: clean, sweet-smelling
Tony: the name became a nickname for 'fool' during the seventeenth century, possibly as a result of its use in this play
He can laugh . . . no beast: the Greek philosopher Aristotle (384–322BC) held that the capacity for laughter was one distinction between man and beast
discretion: ability to discriminate, power of reasoning
guide his own: manage his inheritance
assure you: be assured
no cost want: be no expense spared
magnifico: a magistrate or, by implication, anyone of high authority
shorter: less, lower
wit of constable: constables were proverbially of low intelligence, and frequently good for a joke in a play (see Dull in Shakespeare's *Love's Labour Lost* and Dogberry in his *Much Ado About Nothing*)
serve turn: be sufficient
headborough: deputy constable
beadle: minor parish official
able him: make him fit for
there I would have it: that's just what I would like
go to: all right
passing: very much indeed (from 'surpassing')
state: status, professional position
goes to: (1) make up, (2) visit
parlous: dangerous; hence, dangerously cunning
deep: difficult
serv'd: been suitable for
say't: say it
push-pin: a child's game, used here with sexual innuendo
We three: probably an allusion to a traditional picture of two idiots' heads, the spectator being the third idiot (compare Shakespeare's *Twelfth Night*, II.3.17)

Put's head i'th'pillory: put his head (perhaps Alibius's or Lollio's) in the public pillory, for providing too little bread
crag: neck
wire: whip
permasant: Parmesan cheese
spoil'd him a: spoiled his
***stultus, stulta, stultum*:** in Latin, the masculine, feminine and neuter of 'foolish'

Act II Scene I

The scene now moves to Vermandero's castle. Beatrice is seen sending a letter to Alonzo via Jasperino. Alone, she comments how good a judge is Alsemero in his choice of friends, and she feels that 'I love now with the eyes of judgment' (II.1.13). She does not know how to go about telling her father, who is intent on her speedy marriage to Alonzo de Piracquo.

De Flores enters, unseen by Beatrice. He knows that he is ugly and that she cannot stand the sight of him; yet he resolves to see her as often as possible, whatever the scorn she pours upon him. He wonders how others, more ugly than he, manage to win beautiful women. We learn that, although 'hard fate' has forced him to be a servant, he was born a gentleman. Beatrice notices him, saying aside that 'This ominous ill-fac'd fellow more disturbs me/Than all my other passions' (II.1.53–4). She treats him with the contempt he expects, and this is made worse by the fact that his errand from her father is to give her news of Alonzo de Piracquo's arrival at the castle. She dismisses him brutally. As he goes, he again confirms aside that, despite her attitude, he is still compelled to take every possible opportunity of seeing her, clinging to the fact that ugly men manage to have as lovers beautiful women who had previously shown contempt for them. Beatrice cannot rid herself of the feeling that De Flores is a threat to her, and resolves to make her father dismiss him. Then, as her father enters with Alonzo de Piracquo and his brother, Tomazo de Piracquo, she is presented with a more immediate problem. She begs her father that the marriage be delayed another three days. Vermandero puts the request to Alonzo who says that, despite his disappointment, if it pleases Beatrice then he must agree with gladness. Vermandero and Beatrice exeunt.

Tomazo points out to Alonzo that Beatrice does not seem to welcome her husband-to-be with open arms, and suggests that she may have transferred her affections to another. He advises Alonzo to give up the lady. Alonzo cannot see any of this, complains that Tomazo is imagining things, and warns that he must fall out with his brother if he continues to make such suggestions, for he will consider an enemy anyone who calls Beatrice's honour into question. Alonzo leaves.

Tomazo comments that his brother is suffering from 'love's tame madness' (II.1.154) which will bring trouble upon him.

NOTES AND GLOSSARY:

***severally*:** separately. On the Elizabethan stage they probably entered by different doors
conduct: a paper with directions
Fitness of: the appropriate
set down: written down
I shall return: I shall take back (to Alsemero)
approv'd: confirmed, justified
turns head: her father will turn against her
remember'd: thought up, borne in mind
he's so forward: Alonzo is so eager
my new comforts: Alsemero. The entrance of De Flores here is ironic, since it is he who is to offer Beatrice a different kind of 'comfort' – that of murdering the inconvenient Alonzo
Yonder's she: she is over there
ails: is the matter with
a'late: of late, recently
force: contrive
At no hand: on no account, by no means
far worse: far worse a face
not endur'd alone: not only put up with
pick-hair'd faces: this probably means 'with tufts of hairs and bristles sticking out'
Now't: now it
Thy business? What's thy business?: Middleton creates an atmosphere of great tension during the exchange between Beatrice and De Flores which follows these words. The conversation is barely twenty lines long, but it is made to seem embarrassingly longer by the very short speeches, many only half lines, and by the mixture of open remarks and asides
Soft and fair: gently does it (compare Shakespeare, *Much Ado About Nothing*, V.4.72)
fix'd: immovable, in a trance
standing toad-pool: stagnant pond inhabited by toads. Beatrice probably intends to refer both to his present immobility and to the ugliness of his face
amain: with full force
another since: in addition to the last (see I.1.93)
Do't: do it

The said Alonzo . . .: in the following lines De Flores tries to ingratiate himself with Beatrice by using over-elaborate courtly language, but he only succeeds in irritating her
To be i'th' way still: to be ready at hand again
rail'd at: abused
mad qualm: pang of lust
Garden-bull: bull-baiting took place at Paris Garden, which was situated in Southwark near the Globe theatre
lugg'd baited
chops: mouth and cheeks
discarded: dismissed
addition: additional title
our: Vermandero's sense of his high rank prompts him to use a regal plural
keep the night: it might be expected that Beatrice will 'keep the night' in the sense of 'observe the rites of consummation of the marriage'; in fact, she means just the opposite, that she will 'guard against Alonzo's advances in the night'
ill-set: full of type-setter's errors
faults: errata, list of corrections
pinching: too tight, that is, rather short notice
exceptious: full of objections
cozened: cheated
pleasure: sexual enjoyment
get: beget, father
her restraint may go in time to: will be the eventual result of restraining her natural inclinations
thought on: thought about
and that/Be your fear only: if that is your only fear
that should but think: who could so much as think
yet w'are friends: we are still friends
not myself: not in control of myself
bound: owe it to heaven

Act II Scene 2

Diaphanta brings Alsemero to a place where he and Beatrice can meet secretly. Their happiness is only marred by the existence of Alonzo de Piracquo, and the fact that she is commanded by her father to marry him. Alsemero suggests that he should immediately challenge Alonzo to a duel, but Beatrice can see the foolishness of that course of action: if Alsemero were to win, he would suffer under the law. 'Blood-guiltiness', she says, 'becomes a fouler visage' (II.1.40); at which her mind turns to De Flores. She swiftly conceives a cunning plan, spoken aside and thus not revealed to Alsemero, of using De Flores for her purposes. She regrets that in the past she has not been artful enough, and has alienated De Flores by her scorn. Advising caution for the time being to Alsemero, she instructs Diaphanta to guide him back the secret way that they came. As he leaves, Alsemero reaffirms his unshakeable love.

De Flores enters. He has been spying on the meeting between Beatrice and Alsemero, and observes that if Beatrice is to become promiscuous and entertain men other than her husband, then he'll 'put in for one' (1.60). Beatrice, in an aside, resolves not to show her hatred of De Flores and to speak pleasantly to him in order to bend him to her will. De Flores is overjoyed when, instead of abusing him, Beatrice calls him by his name; says that his face is improving – when he knows 'Tis the same physnomy, to a hair and pimple, /Which she call'd scurvy scarce an hour ago' (11.76–7); she touches his face; promises to prepare an ointment that will cleanse it within a fortnight; and praises rugged features as evidence of toughness. De Flores offers his service in any way she wishes. She sighs, and he hears her call him 'my De Flores', saying that she wished that she were born a man. He kneels, vowing to fulfil any service that she requires. Beatrice thinks that he must be greedy for money, little thinking that the reward he is greedy for is her body. She confides that she hates Alonzo de Piracquo; De Flores replies that he is as good as dead. She urges caution, and promises rich reward and safe-conduct abroad after the deed is done. He replies that they will talk of that later. She thinks that she will be rid of two loathed men at the same time – Alonzo and De Flores. She leaves. De Flores is exultant, already imagining her in his arms.

Alonzo de Piracquo enters and asks De Flores to show him over the fortifications of the castle. De Flores quickly accepts, seizing such an early opportunity to carry out Beatrice's commission.

NOTES AND GLOSSARY:

This is the first of the two scenes (the other is III.4) where the play rises to the level of 'great' drama. There is the panting pace of Beatrice-Joanna as she urges De Flores on to violence, little realising how she is arousing him sexually. There is irony, even comedy, in the fact that both Beatrice and De Flores become increasingly excited about what they see as the imminent fulfilment of their wishes; yet Beatrice and, to some extent, De Flores are both deceived concerning the real intentions of each other. The use of asides shows that each character is operating at a level of inner significance which is isolated from the other – and from reality.

charge:	responsibility
your hour:	the hour of your appointment

just: perfect, just as you could wish
complete: perfect
cabinets: confidantes
'em: gifts in answer to our requests
furnish our defects: supply what we lack
strike off: as one might strike off the fetters of a prisoner
remove the cause,/The command ceases: that is, remove Alonzo de Piracquo and Vermandero's command can have no effect
two fears . . . same blast: as one might blow out two lights with one breath
let me find you: allow me to understand your meaning
'bout: about, which is part of
ventured: risked, at risk
condition: type
ne'er 'a': never have
becomes: is fitting for
And now I think on one: her mind has jumped straight to De Flores
'T: it
done questionless: carried out by De Flores (1) with no questions asked, (2) without doubt
art . . . art: (1) science, (2) cunning
so sure of: so certainly on
t'other: Alonzo
put in for one: apply for a share. This phrase has the same kind of sexual innuendo as 'serv'd' in the previous line
sutler: supplier/provider to an army
look to be: expect to be
rail'd at: abused
put case: suppose
serve my turn upon him: use him for my own purposes. It is ironic that Beatrice chooses the same word that De Flores has just used in line 59. She does indeed 'serve her turn' upon De Flores, for he commits the murder for her; in return for which she finds that she must let De Flores serve his turn upon her in the sexual sense
a'late: of late, recently
Y'have: You have
prun'd: preened (like a bird)
wont: accustomed
amorously: loveable, fit to be loved
physnomy: physiognomy
heat of the liver: the liver was traditionally the seat of violent passions. Beatrice's made-up diagnosis is, ironically, more correct than she supposes

perceiv't: perceive it
amber: sweetly perfumed with ambergris
wash: medicinal wash, ointment
act of pleasure: sexual act
'Twould: it would
e'er: ever
a service/So happy as that mounts to: with a sexual innuendo
on't: of it
excuse for't: denying it
would fain: desires to
'las: alas. It can be seen how many words in this dialogue are cut short. This, along with the brevity of the speeches themselves, helps to give the exchange a breathless expectancy
Nay, that's not it: this half-line provides a brief moment of comic relief for the audience as the atmosphere of tense expectancy builds up
occasion: opportunity
Put it not from me: do not take away from me this chance to serve you
to mean faithfully: to intend honest service
you would say then . . . charge on't: you would say then that I did not act humbly enough when receiving your instructions to carry out the deed
have the work: know what I have to do
forward: courageous
rewarded: that is, than you shall be
I do think of that: he thinks that the preferred reward is sex; and Beatrice little thinks how she is exciting him, and she fails to notice any significance in De Flores's choice of the word 'ravishes' a few lines earlier
Why: why should you need to tell me that?
cast: throw of the dice
his dog-face: she is referring to De Flores
my blood: my lust, sensual desire. It can well be imagined that the blood is pulsing through De Flores's veins at this time, a signal of the arousing of violent passion
Hunger and pleasure . . . Slovenly dishes: Hunger for food and sex are sometimes so acute that women will settle for less than choice dishes
straits: narrow passages
'gainst your lordship's rising: when your lordship is ready to rise from the table
beyond hopes: beyond what I could possibly have hoped for

Act III Scene 1

De Flores is seen conducting Alonzo de Piracquo around the fortifications. Upon the pretext that they should not go down a narrow staircase wearing their swords , De Flores takes off his sword and hangs it up on a hook. Alonzo does likewise. They proceed on their tour.

NOTES AND GLOSSARY:

In the act-time DE FLORES ***hides a naked rapier***: between each act there would have been a short pause in the action, during which the musicians would probably have played some music. In this interval De Flores comes on stage and hides a rapier in full view of the audience

wanted for the postern: not got in my possession the key to the back-door

sconce: small fort

You'll tell me more . . .: that is, because you haven't seen everything yet

Act III Scene 2

De Flores and Alonzo enter upon another battlement. Alonzo mentions that everybody thinks that he is out in a gondola – a piece of information which increases De Flores's sense of safety. While Alonzo is admiring the view, De Flores takes up the rapier that he had previously hidden and stabs him from behind. It is clearly a bloody murder, for De Flores has to stab him repeatedly before he dies. De Flores notices a ring on one of Alonzo's fingers, which he resolves to take to Beatrice as proof that the murder has been carried out. As the ring will not budge, he cuts off the finger, then drags out the body in order to hide it.

NOTES AND GLOSSARY:

A place you little dream on: Alonzo thinks that De Flores is talking of the wonderful fortifications; the audience will appreciate the irony, for De Flores means the grave and possibly, beyond that, heaven or hell

makes up: makes for, completes

dwell: rest the eye upon

upon't: looking at it

approve the work: prove that the assassination has been carried out

suspect: suspicion

Act III Scene 3

In the madhouse, Isabella, Doctor Alibius's wife, is complaining to Lollio about her lack of freedom to go out and about. Lollio explains, in thinly disguised sexual imagery, that his master is afraid of what will happen if she goes gadding about, saying that all sorts of people are to be found within the madhouse, if she wishes to be sociable. She complains that they are all either fools or madmen, but agrees to let Lollio show her the 'pleasure of your bedlam' (III.3.24), particularly one handsome-looking lunatic admitted recently whom Lollio has praised.

Lollio goes out and returns with Franciscus, who, Lollio says, is a poet who has gone mad over his love for a chambermaid. At first Franciscus is gentle and talks of Titania, the Faery Queen, claiming that he is Tiresias, the famous poet. Then he becomes more violent and tries to seize Lollio, who shows him his keeper's whip as a warning that he should calm down. Isabella is frightened and asks for him to be sent away. Franciscus talks of his love in terms of sexual imagery, before being sent away by Lollio.

A fool, Antonio, is allowed in. There is a disturbance among the madmen in the upper room, and Lollio goes off to quell it. At this Antonio immediately drops his pretence of madness and declares that he is a gentleman who is desperately in love with Isabella, and that he has disguised himself as a madman in order to gain access to her. He kisses her. She rejects his advances; but says that she will not give him away, and that when he has had enough of playing the fool he may 'leave the school', for he can expect no further favour from her. Lollio re-enters and offers to remove Antonio, but she asks for him to stay. There is more disturbance from the madmen, and Lollio goes out again. Antonio tries to kiss Isabella again. Lollio re-enters above and sees what is going on below between Antonio and Isabella, perceiving that Alibius will soon be made a cuckold. Madmen enter above, dressed as birds or beasts. Lollio re-enters below. When Isabella says that 'Your fool is grown wonderous witty' (III.3.216), Lollio remarks pointedly that 'he will put you down one of these days' (III.3.218). He then takes Antonio away.

Alone, Isabella comments that now she 'need not gad abroad to seek her sin' (III.3.221). Lollio re-enters, and immediately tries to make love to Isabella, indicating that he knows what is going on between her and Antonio and demanding his share in the amorous sport. She rebuts him, saying that if he breathes a word of what he knows then she will get Antonio to cut his throat as a condition for her yielding her love to him. Lollio persists, but is interrupted by the arrival of Alibius, who has news that Vermandero has commissioned him to present a show of dancing fools and madmen as a finale to the revels which are to be held in celebration of the wedding of Beatrice-Joanna. Lollio declares that he can arrange a good show. Alibius remarks to his wife that it is fools and madmen who provide them with a living.

NOTES AND GLOSSARY:

pipe: sing? co-operate? Lollio is probably making a sly advance to Isabella, suggesting that she might co-operate in 'doing' (1.4)

pinfold: cattle pen

taken in another man's corn: found like a stray cow in another man's field

pounded: (1) impounded, put in a pen; (2) pressed and hammered sexually

to boot: as well

Of either sort one . . : one of you is mad and the other a fool

participate of: share, take part in. Again, Lollio hints at sexual activity

brave: fine

afford: offer

proper: handsome

mirth in madness: that is, by laughing at his plight

match: bargain

sheeting: pulling back

Anacreon: Anacreon (?572–?488 BC), the Greek lyric poet, choked to death on a grape-stone whilst drinking a cup of wine

there's a spider in the cup: in popular belief spiders were poisonous, and to drink one knowingly meant death

the Muses then forsook him: his inspiration deserted him. In Greek mythology the Muses were divine beings who inspired writers

but a dwarf neither: nothing but a dwarf

Titania . . . Oberon: Queen and King of the fairies, whose most famous literary portrayal is in Shakespeare's *A Midsummer Night's Dream* (?1594). Franciscus is suggesting that as Oberon (Alibius) is sporting with his Dryades, or nymphs (other women), Titania (Isabella) should sport with him

Diomed: Thracian king who fed his horses on human flesh

Bucephalus: Alexander the Great's (356–323 BC) huge horse, which only he could ride. Franciscus is inviting Lollio to climb on his back like a rider

Esculapius: Greek god of medicine, a name which Franciscus here ironically gives to Lollio

poison: the whip

Tiresias: in Greek mythology a Theban prophet who changed from a man to a woman and then, seven years later, back to a man. As a punishment for revealing that women enjoyed sexual intercourse more than men he was struck blind by the goddess Juno

tame wild-geese: slang term for prostitutes

make no words on't: don't talk about it

eye: that is, pudendum

Luna: the moon, which was responsible for lunacy

two trades to beg with: blindness and madness were considered two qualifications for begging

Hecate: Greek goddess of witchcraft and magic, associated with the moon

kick the dog and beat the bush: traditionally the man in the moon owned a dog and a bush (compare Shakespeare's *A Midsummer Night's Dream*, V.1.249–50)

lie: that is, with sexual intent

mouse-hole: again, the pudendum

aunt: slang for mistress, prostitute or bawd

nidget: a form of 'idiot'

bauble (1) a stick surmounted by a carved ass's head and traditionally carried by a court fool, (2) penis

cousin: in Jacobean times, not just an indication of blood relationship, but an expression of intimate friendship; hence Isabella's reaction in the following line

so much wit as: enough wit

left-handed: clumsy

Orlando: the fierce, mad fighter, hero of *Orlando Furioso* (1516) by the Italian author Ludovico Ariosto (1474–1533)

amazing: amazed

scrutinous: investigative

mystery: deep knowledge or skill

parlous: dangerous, cunning

forward: presumptuous

fashion'd out: devised, invented

Galaxia: Milky Way

acquaintance: notice

Passing: very

come to something: possibly Isabella intends a sexual innuendo; yet it must be meant ironically, as he has made no progess with her

put him to't: test him

catch the last couple in hell: a reference to the game of 'barley-brake', where one couple begins by holding the middle ground, called 'hell'. They catch other couples attempting to run through, who then assist the original pair until the last couple has been caught (compare V.3.162–3). Clearly, the game was sometimes used as an exciting mating ritual

out again: out of your role as madman again

posture: pose

from your clothes: not in accordance with the way you are dressed

orchard of the Hesperides: a mythical orchard situated beyond the edge of the western world, where golden apples grew

pull: pick, pluck

venter: venture, try

giants keep 'em: in Greek mythology the orchard of the Hesperides was guarded by giants; the Hesperides were nymphs appointed to guard the golden apples Gē gave to Hera on the day of her marriage to Zeus

Lipsius: Justus Lipsius (1547–1606), a Belgian Neo-Stoic scholar, whose name is used here merely to make a pun on 'lips'

***Ars Amandi*:** *Art of Love*, the Roman poet Ovid's (43BC–?AD17) treatise on the art of seduction

Do you smile: simply means 'smile'

Look you but cheerfully: if you will only look happy

mirrors: Isabella's eyes

cuckoo: a call implying that Alibius is about to be cuckolded

conceit: fancy

These are no fears: there is nothing to fear in these mad people

two beneficiaries at once: a reference to the widespread abuse of increasing a churchman's wages by allowing him to hold more than one living (to be in charge of more than one church)

play'd: even this word has sexual overtones

I do not think but: I can only think that

put you down: (1) beat you in a witty argument, (2) lie on top of you and make love to you

bankers: builders of dykes; here referring to Alibius and Lollio

would a woman: if a woman wanted to

needle's point will to the fixed north: the point of the compass is inevitably drawn to the magnetic north of women's beauty. Probably also a sexual allusion to the erection of the penis

a thing about thee: her pudendum

purchase: gaining, achieving

his injunction/For me enjoying: the task I shall give him, the reward for which will be my giving myself to him sexually.

These lines suggest a direct parallel with the main plot

bounden: (1) faithful, (2) imprisoned

fag: end, conclusion

the third night from the first: of three whole nights

an unexpected passage over: a sudden, brief interlude

a frightful pleasure: a light-hearted fright

Y'ave: You have

lawyer's haven: the prosperous 'harbour of the lawyer', who thrives on those foolish or mad enough to go to law

Act III Scene 4

Vermandero is taking Alsemero round the castle. He likes Alsemero, saying that he wishes he had another daughter for him, but that Beatrice's sister has died. Left alone, Beatrice expresses pleasure that Alsemero is finding favour with her father.

De Flores enters, and informs Beatrice that 'Piracquo is no more' (III.4.23). She is delighted at the news, then horrified when he shows her the finger with the ring on it. He wonders why she should react to this more than at news of 'killing the whole man' (III.4.30). The ring was, she says, the first token that her father made her send to Alonzo de Piracquo; she assures De Flores of its value, saying that he may have it. He remarks that it will hardly cover his conscience at the killing. She says that she did not intend that to be his reward. He hopes that indeed it is not. She offers him three thousand gold florins. He rejects these 'wages'. She does not understand, and offers to double the sum. She is becoming frightened and urges him to flee, telling him to write down on paper the sum he requires if he is too 'modest' to name it to her face. He says that they are together in the plot, and if he is to run away then she must go with him. At last it dawns upon her what he desires, but she dares not even admit that she realises his aim; so he has to tell her plainly that, though he desires gold, he desires more the pleasure of enjoying her virginity. She protests that he cannot be so wicked as 'to make his [Alonzo's] death the murderer of my honour!' (III.4.122); to which he justly replies: 'Push, you forget yourself!'/A woman dipp'd in blood, and talk of modesty!' (III.4.125–6). She now wishes that she had settled for a hateful marriage, and appeals to De Flores to recognise the differences in their births. He scornfully points out that their consciences are equals, telling her that she is 'the deed's creature' (III.4.137), a murderess and villain like him. If she does not submit to his lust, he says that he will confess all, careless of his life. She kneels to him and offers all her wealth; he replies that all the wealth of Valencia 'shall not buy/My pleasure from me' (III.4.159–60). She despairs, seeing that

'Murder . . . is followed by more sins' (III.4.164). He raises her up and holds her close to him, saying 'Thou'lt love anon/What thou so fear'st and faint'st to venture on' (III.4.170–1).

NOTES AND GLOSSARY:

This is justifiably the most famous scene in the play, where De Flores comes to Beatrice for his reward. As in II.2 the dialogue between Beatrice and De Flores consists of broken verse, with short sentences and speeches which are sometimes bare half-lines, giving the impression of breathless expectancy – at least, this is so early in the scene. After about line 105 the speeches become longer as De Flores asserts his dominance and Beatrice is broken down.

this creature: Beatrice; but he does not use the word in any derogatory sense

But Heaven has married her . . .: she is dead and in Heaven

'Twere: it were

this vale: this life is referred to as a 'vale of tears'

largely: widely spoken about

fix him: that is, in my father's favour

that eye: Alonzo's

I could not get the ring without the finger: perhaps symbolic of the impossibility of Beatrice's truly cutting herself free from her betrothal to Alonzo. See also line 38

A greedy hand . . .: a finger has been cut off in the rush for food

keeper: game-keeper

on shortly: of soon

'Twill: it will

capcase: case, covering, small container

worm: worm of conscience, which causes gnawing remorse

my merit/Would scorn the way on't: my great worth would lead me to despise that way of gaining reward

In state of: by way of

were much: would be rather presumptuous

journeyman in murder: hired assassin

brought home: accomplished

suspect: suspicion

speaks home: brings the truth of the matter home to me

What makes: why is

strange: unfriendly, unwilling

doubt: fear

pain: the pain of sexual longing

Soft: wait a minute, not so fast

wrought myself into't: worked to have the task given to me

In order: in due course

held: considered
resolv'd: certain
keep thee there: that is, in your place
Fly not to your birth, but settle you/In . . .: do not rush to protect yourself by mentioning your high birth, but resign yourself to . . .
no more: no higher
forget your parentage to me: forget your station in life when dealing with me
first condition: innocence
made you one with: made you inseparable from
urge me: provoke me (to use plainer words)
he's chang'd now: he, Alonzo, is now a changeling in that he is dead
bring thy second on: that is, with sexual innuendo
sweets that ever darkness tasted: delightful sexual activity that has ever taken place in the dark
enjoy: that is, sexually
I shall rest . . . then: I shall not suffer sexual longings when I am dead
Vengeance: in this case, apparently, divine retribution
with a viper first: with an unnatural being before a normal man
receipts: recipes
turtle: turtle-dove
anon: at once, very quickly (as with 'presently', this word has become weakened over the centuries, and now means merely 'soon')

Act IV Scene I

The beginning of this scene is a dumb-show (in which the action is mimed and there is no talking). Vermandero is seen expressing wonder at the apparent flight of Alonzo de Piracquo. He decrees that Alsemero shall supply his place and marry Beatrice, to general approval. Beatrice crosses the stage, dressed as a bride and attended by her women. De Flores follows, smiling – until the ghost of Alonzo appears to him, showing his hand where a finger is missing. All depart and the dumb-show ends.

Beatrice re-enters alone. Clearly, De Flores has by now deflowered her, and she views with horror the coming night's love-making in the bridal bed. She fears that she can never hide the loss of her virginity from Alsemero, and considers that it would be only just if he were to strangle her as she lies by him. As she soliloquises, she comes upon a closet used by Alsemero, with the key in the lock. She opens it, and is alarmed to find inside, along with miscellaneous chemicals, vials and medical apparatus, instructions designed to discover whether a woman is pregnant. Even more disturbing is a second set of instructions designed to find out whether or not a woman is a maid. Upon administering the relevant potion, a true maid will apparently first yawn, then sneeze, then laugh.

Diaphanta enters. She jokes in a bawdy fashion about Beatrice's approaching wedding night, but Beatrice reproves her, saying that she is so apprehensive that she would give a thousand ducats to any genuine maid who would take her place and then report to her the next day what the losing of virginity was like. Diaphanta finds it hard to believe that Beatrice will forgo her first night's pleasure, and give money too; and declares, as Beatrice expected, that she herself would like to fill Beatrice's place. Beatrice tries out on Diaphanta the potion designed to test virginity: Diaphanta yawns, then sneezes, then laughs, and finally settles into a melancholy mood. It is agreed that Diaphanta shall take Beatrice's place in the nuptial bed, but will leave it at about midnight so that Beatrice can slip into bed beside Alsemero.

NOTES AND GLOSSARY:

Many critics feel that the play deteriorates from the beginning of Act IV. In fact, what deteriorates is not the play, but Beatrice's ability to hold the situation together (compare Macbeth's problems after the murder of Duncan from the beginning of Act III in Shakespeare's *Macbeth* (?1606)). Now that Beatrice and De Flores understand one another and are in league, the struggle moves from a psychological level to one of intrigue and plotting. Alsemero is now 'on the other side', a potential enemy who must be outmanoeuvred; and the virginity test, while rather absurd, is a symbol of the kind of moral trap that awaits to ensnare Beatrice now that she is a fallen women. In this scene we see how she is prepared to use Diaphanta just as earlier she set out to use De Flores.

***accident*:** incident, event
undone me endlessly: (1) seduced and repeatedly made love to me, (2) damned me eternally
on't: of it
grow up: increase
precious: difficult, skilful
die: one of a pair of dice
right: proper
physic: medicine
great man's wisdom: because great men might fear being poisoned
***Secrets in Nature*:** Antonius Mizaldus (1520–78) wrote a book with this title (*De Arcanis Naturae*). There are no pregnancy or virginity tests in it, but they are to be found in another book by the same author
break you: that is, glass C

turn you into milk: replace you with milk
look to you: watch out for you
Belike: perhaps
never yet made proof: it has never yet been put to the test
several: separate
incontinently: without control
heavy: sluggish
Where had I been?: what would have become of me if he had tested me and I had not discovered this?
Cuds: a contracted form of 'God save us'
nice piece: scrupulous woman indeed (whom)
to look: to look for
rangers: game wardens
a little lodge: with a sexual quibble on woman's pudendum
pit-hole: (1) grave, (2) pudendum
set light by: make light of
ow'd: owned
Do you mean good sooth . . .?: are you in earnest?
upon the fear at first: of my fears when the question of marriage first arose
try what my fear were: put my fear to the test
get: find, procure
lies: (1) makes love, (2) deceives
humour: fancy, whim
by-bet to wedge in the honour: an added inducement to get her to bargain her honour
quick: eager
urge: provoke
ay: yes
praise itself: show its value
it stirs me not a whit, which most concerns it: it does not affect me at all, whose lack of virginity it is its concern to detect
Just: accurate
circumscrib'd: specific in the effects laid down for it
accident: symptom
lays itself: disperses its effects, subsides
carriage: performance, handling
burthen: burden, that is, of a man
I'm for a justice now . . . small fools: now I've enough of a dowry (portion) to make me eligible for a great fool, namely, a justice

Act IV Scene 2

It is now suspected that Alonzo de Piracquo has been murdered. Two gentlemen of Vermandero's household, Antonio and Franciscus, apparently both left the castle at about the time Alonzo disappeared, and Vermandero sends out a warrant for their arrest. Tomazo de Piracquo appears, and accuses Vermandero of responsibility for Alonzo's disappearance; Vermandero counters by blaming Alonzo for departing so suddenly and tells Tomazo to leave the castle.

Vermandero departs. Tomazo determines on some kind of revenge. He talks to De Flores who, uneasy in his mind at being close to the man whose brother he has murdered, makes an excuse to get away as soon as possible. Ironically, Tomazo concludes: 'That De Flores has a wondrous honest heart' (IV.2.57). Alsemero enters, and Tomazo frankly tells him that he suspects that Alsemero has taken his brother's place by foul play. They exchange hard words, and threaten that next time they meet they will fight. Tomazo exits. Alsemero's wedding day is disturbed further when his friend Jasperino tells him that Beatrice and De Flores have been overheard having an intimate conversation; this is particularly strange as it is believed that Beatrice cannot bear the sight of De Flores. Alsemero can scarcely credit what he hears. He sends Jasperino to get the virginity potion from his chest. Diaphanta has told him of Beatrice's fears at losing her virginity, and when Beatrice now appears her modesty supports this; but he feels that he 'cannot be too sure' (IV.2.126). When Jasperino returns carrying the glass bottle with M inscribed thereon, Beatrice recognises it as the virginity test potion and knows that she is suspected. Alsemero gives her the potion to drink, whereupon she pretends first to yawn, then to sneeze, and then to laugh, finally settling into a melancholy mood. Alsemero is overjoyed that she is 'proved' a maid, and embraces 'My Joanna,/Chaste as the breath of Heaven' (IV.2.148–9).

NOTES AND GLOSSARY:

The time accuses 'em: they left about the time the murder took place
answer faithfully: explain with confidence
apprehension: arrest
set on: harassed, pestered
bloods: relatives, or perhaps simply followers
the prepar'd morning: the wedding morning for which all was prepared
Whose belief hurt 'em: whose faith in him caused them to be hurt
one of his alliance: one of his family, or, anyone connected with him
fain get off: like to get away
brings it so fresh: brings it back so vividly
jealousy: suspicion
at no hand: by no means

th'are: they are
salute: consort with, keep the company of
o'erlays my conscience: oppresses my thoughts
reckons: settle our scores (possibly by fighting)
more precious liquor: blood
lay: allay, quench
I'll have it ready drawn: that is, my sword, with a pun on the drawing up of words as a formal answer
Keep your day solemn: celebrate the solemnities of your wedding
so my faith . . .: provided that/if it were possible that my faith . . .
dispense a little . . . cool in this: allow the keenness of my friendship towards you to cool a little so that I do not have to give you this news
puts me on: provokes my curiosity
No question: without question
pretend: offer
out: mistaken
prevent: forestall
made me stagger: gave me a shock
challenge interest: claim rights
dangerous to thy bosom: that is, I may stab you
touch'd: tainted
weigh me by my passions: judge me by my outburst of passion
Chaldean: an astrologer or soothsayer (see the Bible, Daniel 2:2)
Deliver'd her for: described her as
obscurely: in darkness
composition: mixture, concoction
warrant: guarantee

Act IV Scene 3

The scene is the madhouse. Isabella reads to Lollio a love letter from the madman Franciscus which shows that he, too, is only pretending to be mad in order to gain access to her. They agree to have some fun with these 'counterfeit madmen', but Lollio warns Isabella that if she gives in to them, then he himself will 'put in for my thirds' (IV.3.37) and 'fall upon you' (IV.341). Alibius enters, eager to know whether all is ready for the show at Vermandero's castle the following evening. Lollio says that the fools are reliable enough, but he does not trust the madmen. Alibius is worried that they will frighten the ladies, but Lollio assures him that he can control the situation. Alibius enquires how his wife is putting up with the restrictions placed upon her, and says that she shall accompany the party to Vermandero's castle, which is enough liberty for her for another month. Lollio makes an allusion to the fact that Alibius is in danger of being made a cuckold, but Alibius does not understand, thinking that Lollio is indulging in some tomfoolery. Alibius goes out.

Lollio summons Antonio in order to teach him to dance. Isabella enters, dressed like a madwoman, and hangs upon Antonio. Irritated, he tries to disengage himself from her, letting slip his madman's manner of speaking. She then reveals herself to him, saying that because he has failed to prove a 'quick-sighted lover' (IV.3.137) and so see through her disguise, she rejects him. She goes out. Lollio re-enters. Antonio abandons his disguise altogether and threatens to beat Lollio, who says that he saw through him long ago; but he assures Antonio that his mistress loves him, and reveals that there is another 'counterfeit madman' in the house whom Isabella does not love. If he, Antonio, can get rid of the other 'madman', then she will submit to his love. Antonio, despite doubts, is taken in by Lollio. He then exits.

Franciscus, Antonio's rival, enters. Lollio shows him that he has his love letter and knows that he is only pretending to be mad. Franciscus bribes Lollio to advance his suit. Lollio says that his mistress loves Franciscus, but requires proof of his love for her which he can give her by confronting her enemy and his rival after the masque at Vermandero's castle. They are interrupted by Alibius, who has come to see the final rehearsal for the masque. The madmen and fools perform their dance, and Alibius is satisfied that all is perfect and that the performance will bring credit and money to them.

NOTES AND GLOSSARY:

his inside with his out: the contents of the letter which show his real nature compared with his outward behaviour in the madhouse

Andromeda: Isabella

chambermaid: chambermaids were traditionally promiscuous

Scorpio, in the middle region: the sign of Scorpio governed the genitals

the bellows-mender of Aeolus: Lollio. Middleton seems to equate bellows-menders with bawds

privy to your skill: that is, know what is going on

minister once and set up the trade: once give yourself to another and thus become a whore

thirds: a third share, after Alibius and her lover

I shall be mad or fool else: that is, I would be crazy to miss the opportunity

I stand to my venture: I will stand by my side of the bargain. 'Stand' is also a common Elizabethan pun for the erection of the penis

deal: (1) cope, (2) have sexual intercourse

the fair understanding: taking my words in the decent sense
use: treat
kindly: (1) kindly, (2) according to their natures
practise: trick them
fit . . . fit: dress . . . prepare
Take thou no further notice than the outside: that is, behave as if I were a madwoman
close up the solemnity: conclude the wedding celebrations
so: provided that
rough behaviours/Affright the ladies: compare Quince's worries in *A Midsummer Night's Dream* (?1595), (I.2.72–4)
pizzles: dried bulls' penises used as whips
morris: morris dance
let me alone: trust me
measure: dance
more length: that is, more rope, a little more freedom
the trunk of a young elephant: either an allusion to the horns that cuckolds were supposed to grow from their foreheads, or a suggestion that Alibius is being led by the nose
footmanship: dancing steps
ride: with sexual innuendo
Vault in: jump in to the dance
honour: bow
Caper: a dance consisting of leaps in the air
figure: (1) set of dancing movements, (2) appearance
Icarus: in Greek mythology, when Icarus flew too near the sun the wax melted which held on his wings
Dedalus: creator of the labyrinth in Crete in which the Minotaur lived. He was the father of Icarus
lower labyrinth: probably intended as a sexual allusion
drown'd: after his wings were gone, according to the legend Icarus fell into the sea and drowned
turbant: turban
reversion of: right to succeed to
antic: clown, buffoon
frantic: mad person
caparisons: coverings, clothes
usher: door-keeper, junior teacher
coxcomb: idiot
forbear: spare
fox-skin: cunning disguise
arrant: absolute
ride: mount sexually

She's eased . . . quarrel on't: she shall be rid of him; I have a good reason to pick a quarrel with him
station: status (of a fool)
like: likely
Latona: mother of Diana, the huntress; although Diana herself seems to be meant here
this trick, and another that I know: deception, and adultery
yours: that is, your handwriting, your letter
pick: pick my pocket
it does lie: that is, your letter
give you over: hand you over (to Isabella)
cast your water: have your urine examined
well-favouredly: soundly
one incurable fool/That might be begg'd?: to beg a fool was to gain appointment as his guardian in order to have the use of his money
fit: prepare perfectly

Act V Scene 1

The scene moves back to the castle. The clock strikes one, Beatrice is anxiously waiting for Diaphanta to return from the bridal bed. She feels that she cannot now trust Diaphanta, who, she also thinks, may have been responsible for Alsemero suspecting her chastity; hence, she will kill her. The clock strikes two. De Flores enters. Day is coming and all will be discovered soon if Diaphanta does not come. De Flores conceives a plan: he will start a fire in Diaphanta's chamber which will rouse the house. Then if Diaphanta is found far from her room, it will be put down to her fright of the fire. If she returns to her room unseen, De Flores will kill her there with an explosive charge, which he will claim was fired up the chimney in Diaphanta's room in order to make sure that the fire is blown out. Beatrice admires this cunning so much that she now feels that she loves De Flores indeed – as he had predicted at the end of III.4. The ghost of Alonzo appears briefly to De Flores and Beatrice. De Flores goes out.

The clock strikes three. Shouts of 'Fire!' begin, an alarm bell rings, frantic activity ensues and De Flores is seen directing operations. Beatrice delights in the speed and skill with which he works, declaring that 'Here's a man worth loving' (V.1.76).

Diaphanta enters, to be met curtly by Beatrice and sent to her chamber for her reward. Alsemero enters, going swiftly to reassure Beatrice, who he thinks has followed him from his bed. Vermandero and Jasperino enter. De Flores crosses the stage with a loaded firepiece, saying that he is taking it to 'scour the chimney' in Diaphanta's room.

Vermandero and Beatrice join in commending his excellent presence of mind. The firepiece is heard to go off, and Beatrice knows that Diaphanta is dead; but she pretends to be anxious for her. De Flores re-enters with the bad news that Diaphanta has been burnt to death in the fire. Alsemero begs Beatrice not to distress herself further. A servant enters to announce that the fire is out. Beatrice commands De Flores to see to the burial of Diaphanta's body, and she says that he ought to be rewarded for his discovery of the fire and his skill in dealing with it. Vermandero agrees, and tells De Flores to come and see him. Alsemero, too, wishes to reward him.

All depart except for De Flores, who now in turn admires Beatrice's female trickery which has gained him rewards for villainy.

NOTES AND GLOSSARY:

Beatrice and De Flores now recognise one another as equals, and in this scene we see them admiring each other's cunning. The contrived, even absurd, situation allows us to accept the more credible change in the relationship between Beatrice and De Flores. This scene well illustrates the close nature of the Middleton–Rowley collaboration. Beatrice's tension and De Flores' reactions to the situation are typical of Middleton; the violent action later in the scene feels more like Rowley's creation. Dorothy Farr's note on this scene is relevant here:

> The scene in which Beatrice, shivering in her night-gown, waits for Diaphanta to come from her bridegroom so that she may take her place, is built upon a crescendo of anxiety. Beatrice is like a taut string and De Flores plays upon her, while the striking clocks, punctuating their whispered conversation, suggest the night stillness as well as the passage of time .... Against the pleasant dawn associations the significance of what the first daylight can mean for Beatrice links back to her dread of Alsemero's 'clear understanding'.*

by't: by it, that is, through it, still

No trusting of her life: there is no way she can be trusted alive

the devil . . . his itch: presumably, uncontrollable lust

termagants: shrewish, wilful women

fall upon: go to bed with

game royal: hunting game in the royal grounds

Then: for, moreover

fall'n off: withdrawn

Phosphorus: the Greek word for the morning star. The Latin equivalent is Lucifer, which is another name for Satan. Hence, De Flores is associated with the Devil

*Dorothy M. Farr, *Thomas Middleton and the Drama of Realism*, Oliver and Boyd, Edinburgh, 1973, p.57.

fall upon some ruin: hit upon some desperate plan of action
force a rising: get everybody out of bed
no remedy: no other remedy
give over all: give up all hope
reach: plan
light parcels: small items
is now: in normal circumstances, when there is no fire
piece: fowling piece, heavily loaded shotgun
As 'twere to cleanse the chimney: A crude but effective way of cleaning a chimney, and thus putting out a chimney fire, was to fire a gun loaded with shot up it
mark: target
'Slid: by God's eyelid
Our pleasure and continuance: our continued sexual pleasure
by Saint Sebastian's: by the clock at Saint Sebastian's church
The east is not more beauteous: ironically, the day star, sometimes called Lucifer, has risen in the East
works: burns
charge: powder and shot for his gun
Your reward: Diaphanta expects the thousand ducats; Beatrice means death
prithee tremble not: Alsemero is, of course, quite unaware of the real apprehensions which cause Beatrice to tremble
Dog at: very competent at (like a dog in pursuit)
countenanc'd: saw, employed
heavy: slovenly
mine: dangerous situation (which Beatrice does not make specific)
And they be ne'er so good: however good they are in other respects
What's that?: perhaps De Flores carries some burnt but recognisable garment belonging to Diaphanta
tie: bind. She is playing the part of the obedient wife
throughly: thoroughly
Precious!: Priceless/What a joke!
a trick beyond me: a better trick than I could have managed
sport: (1) physical recreation, (2) sexual intercourse

Act V Scene 2

This scene takes place either in the castle or nearby. Tomazo soliloquises in the style of a melancholy and discontented man. He wants revenge against somebody for the loss of his brother, but he does not know who is responsible, and hence thinks every man he meets is a villain. De Flores crosses the stage and goes out. Tomazo wonders whether so ugly a man can be 'honest', as all men call De Flores. He now instinctively mistrusts him, and feels that he could pick a quarrel with him given the least excuse. Yet any sword that drew his blood would, he imagines, be poisoned, and must be thrown away. When De Flores re-enters, Tomazo strikes him. Both men draw their swords. De Flores, imagining that he sees 'his brother's wounds/Fresh bleeding' (V.2.32–3), cannot strike back at Tomazo and departs, privately considering that Tomazo has some instinct about him, and resolving to avoid him in the future.

Alone, Tomazo renounces friendship with all men until he finds his brother's murderer; otherwise he may be friendly with the murderer himself and not know it. Vermandero, Alibius and Isabella enter. Vermandero greets Tomazo, but he rejects his advances. Vermandero tells Tomazo that his brother's murderers, Antonio and Franciscus, have been discovered in Doctor Alibius's madhouse. Tomazo thanks Vermandero and begs his forgiveness, vowing that he will make the murderers suffer.

NOTES AND GLOSSARY:

wont: used, accustomed

in whom my wrath should settle: towards whom I should direct my anger

methinks: it seems to me

hard bested: hard put to it. Tomazo's attitude has changed since IV.2 in a dramatically unconvincing way. The playwrights seem aware of this fact themselves, as shown in De Flores's aside in V.2.38–42

pest-house: hospital for those suffering from the plague or other infectious disease

contrariety in nature/Betwixt: instinctive emnity between

the least occasion/Would give me game upon him: the slightest provocation would cause me to quarrel and fight with him

made account of: prized, valued

fresh bleeding: perhaps alluding to the popular belief that a murdered man's wounds bleed afresh in the presence of the murderer

in a crystal: quite clearly, as in a crystal ball

question this: take up the issue of why you are attacking me

lodge: that is, where instinct dwells

He came near me now: that is, near to sensing my guilt

not so much/As . . . lock up: I won't even respond to common courtesies

troth: truth

peace . . . calm: that which comes from knowing the identity of the murderers

a'this hand . . . a't'other: on the one hand . . . on the other

justly: exactly
wrought out their leaves: contrived to gain leave to go
conduct: guide

Act V Scene 3

At the castle, Jasperino has reported to Alsemero that Beatrice has again been seen leaving a secret meeting with De Flores. Jasperino exits. Beatrice enters. Alsemero confronts her directly with his doubts about her honesty, and then calls her a whore. He asks why she is now reconciled to De Flores, whom she once hated, and says that Diaphanta witnessed her meeting with him. She denies adultery, and in order to prove her love to him confesses that she is a murderess for his sake, and tells how she employed De Flores to carry out the deed. Alsemero says that he feared this, and views Beatrice with horror. He locks her in his closet while he thinks what to do.

De Flores enters. Alsemero confronts him with the truth, saying that Beatrice has confessed to the murder, and that they shall both die for it. De Flores cheerfully adds that she is a whore. She cries from within the closet that it is a lie. Alsemero thrusts De Flores in to join her.

Vermandero, Alibius, Isabella, Tomazo, Franciscus and Antonio enter. Although it is not made clear in the text, presumably Franciscus and Antonio are under guard. Vermandero tries to tell Alsemero that the murderers are discovered, but Alsemero interrupts him to say that he knows who are the real murderers. Tomazo grows impatient and angry. Screams are heard from the closet, which Alsemero unlocks. De Flores brings in Beatrice, who is wounded. She refuses to let her father approach her, lest she contaminate him with her vileness. She confesses to Alsemero that she never slept with him, and that her place was supplied by Diaphanta, who died for it. De Flores adds with relish that while Alsemero was with Diaphanta, he, De Flores, 'coupled with your mate/At barley-break' (V.3.162–3). He explains that he loved Beatrice, despite her scorn, and won her love by murdering Alonzo de Piracquo. Vermandero wants De Flores kept alive 'for further tortures' (V.3.172), but De Flores kills himself with his penknife, urging Beatrice to die quickly and follow him – which she does. The only consolation that Alsemero can offer is that the truth is now out and that justice has been done. Tomazo is satisfied, picturing in his mind the murderers now surrounded by the vengeance of hell. Alsemero comments on all the changes that have taken place – in Beatrice, De Flores, Tomazo and himself. Antonio and Franciscus also explain how they came to be changelings. Alibius, at his wife's urging, says that he will change from being a jealous husband. Alsemero urges Vermandero to be consoled, offering him 'a son's duty' (V.3.216).

Alsemero then comes forward and speaks the epilogue to the audience. All consolation is to no purpose, he says, unless the audience approve the play. He implies that if they show their approval, 'all griefs are reconcil'd' (V.3.227).

NOTES AND GLOSSARY:

The final scene shows how justice is dealt out to Beatrice and De Flores in the end, and we hear an assessment of the activities of many of the characters. The significance of what has happened is made clear. This closing scene is probably by Rowley.

The black mask: Beatrice's façade of utter loathing of De Flores
Touch it home: probe to the heart of the matter
Do you laugh?: Alsemero would have expected outraged shock, not laughter, from a truly honest woman
vault: vault of heaven
ground whereon: reason why
ticklish: lascivious
became: suited
despite: detested object
Is there the cause?: Is that the reason?
serpent: that is, De Flores, reminding us of Satan in the form of a snake when Eve was corrupted in the Garden of Eden
blood: sexual longing
the right one: religious devotion to God
'twill have it now: the place (the temple) will have its vengeance (see, for ironic comparison, Alsemero's opening speech of the play, I.1.1–12)
bridge of blood: the murder of Alonzo which has allowed the bridge of marriage to be built between us
ask pause: take time to consider
yet: for the time being. Perhaps Alsemero alludes to the traditional role of the husband as one who 'keeps' the wife
put me in: given me the cue as to where to start
has her commended to you: sends her compliments to you
out: washed out
perceiv'd: a word that suggests something that can be seen and understood with the mind, if not with the eye
behindhand with: indebted to
brave: fine
crying crocodile: it was thought that the crocodile shed hypocritical tears while it was devouring its prey
the black audience/Where: that is, in hell

Clip: embrace
Mare Mortuum: (1) the Dead Sea, which was thought to be bottomless, (2) the bottomless pit of hell
close: impenetrably
acquit them: that is, Vermandero's followers, Antonio and Franciscus
bandied: trifled with
in blood: because I am a blood relation to the murdered man
adultery: Tomazo does not at this point know of the affair between Beatrice and De Flores; thus, he must be looking on Beatrice's marriage to Alsemero as a kind of adultery after her binding betrothal to Alonzo
'tis coming to you: Alonzo's 'recompense for murder and adultery' (see V.3.138)
I'll along for company: De Flores intends to kill himself too
stout: strong
that broken rib of mankind: Eve, the first woman, whose temptation by Satan led to the Fall of Man
I am that . . . better health: an allusion to the practice of opening a vein and draining blood from a patient in order to assist in his cure
common shewer take if from distinction: main drain (sewer) swallow up its identity
yon meteor: De Flores, over there. Meteors were supposed to have an evil influence on mankind's affairs
barley-brake: see note on 'catch the last couple in hell', p. 33
it circumscribes here: Vermandero sees them all within the central area called 'hell' in the game of barley-brake
her heart: which loathed me and loved another
pledge: drink with
taken to thee: this wound I have just given myself (which keeps faith with the one I gave you)
record: the record kept in heaven of human deeds and misdeeds
quit: acquitted, cleared of suspicion
Those black fugitives that are fled from thence: the damned souls of Beatrice and De Flores which have flown from their bodies
Deeper than mine: that is, in hell
opacous: clouded, hence, ominous
master-sin, imperious: murder is considered to be the height of crime
paid before: punished already
Your change: Alonzo's

knowing friendship: knowing who your friends are
on's: of us
innocence: (1) guiltlessness, (2) idiocy (idiots could not be held criminally responsible)
behind: to come
break your own head: put cuckold's horns upon your head
apparent: clearly
Epilogue: this amounts to the conventional plea in Elizabethan epilogues for applause from the audience
stay: check and relieve
Your only: only your
rooms: places

Part 3

Commentary

The Changeling is Middleton's masterpiece, and this is probably due in part to the flair of his collaborator, Rowley. Powerful, economic, straightforward and uncomplicated, the scenes are drawn with restraint and there is nothing wasted. The play is not a 'grand' tragedy; the participants are ordinary people who have to face the consequences of their unconsidered actions. Nonetheless, as a tragedy the drama is only surpassed among the works of Middleton's contemporaries by Shakespeare's tragedies. The following three quotations, drawn from the past one hundred years, may help to serve as an introduction to critical opinion on the play. Swinburne is adoring, Eliot is forthright, and Farr paints a fascinating little picture which highlights the gap between illusion and reality, between what the characters think they are and what they really are.

> Had *The Changeling* not been preserved, we should not have known Middleton: as it is, we are more than justified in asserting that a critic who denies him a high place among the poets of England must be not merely ignorant of the qualities which involve a right or confer a claim to this position, but incapable of curing his ignorance by any process of study.*

> ... there is no doubt about *The Changeling.* Like all of the plays attributed to Middleton, it is long-winded and tiresome; the characters talk too much, and then suddenly stop talking and act; they are real and impelled irresistibly by the fundamental motions of humanity to good or evil. The mixture of tedious discourse and sudden reality is everywhere in the work of Middleton. . . . In reading *The Changeling* we may think, till almost the end of the play, that we have been concerned merely with a fantastic Elizabethan morality, and then discover that we are looking on at a dispassionate exposure of fundamental passions of any time and any place. The usual opinion remains the just judgment: *The Changeling* is Middleton's greatest play.†

> Beatrice is presented like a princess in a fairy tale, only child of a kindly and influential father, with an eager suitor, a secret lover, a

*Algernon Swinburne, Introduction to the Mermaid edition of plays of Thomas Middleton, Vizetelly, London, 1887, p. xxxviii.

†T. S. Eliot, *Elizabethan Dramatists*, Faber, London, 1963, pp. 84–5.

useful confidante and, withal, a waiting gentleman who adores her from his inferior station; Beatrice is the conventional fortunate child, set admist the stage properties of romance. Even the less pleasant elements of the story – the strange closet with its half magical potions with which Alsemero tries to test her chastity, and the substitute bride on the wedding night – are all part of the charming fairy tale in which later De Flores supplies the role of the ogre. Step by step this dream world is unbuilt, and Beatrice herself, shorn little by little of her adolescent naivety, is brought ever closer the man she abhors and the reality that he embodies.*

The setting

George Gascoigne's play *Supposes* began the fashion for Mediterranean settings, and after this many plays, both comedies and tragedies, were set there. To the Elizabethan, the Mediterranean meant all that was foreign, exotic, mysterious. It was idealised as a place of sun, love and beauty – but it was also condemned as one of intrigue, violence and sudden death. It was considered that the southern heat engendered luxury and lust. Anything could happen in such a highly charged atmosphere. Most Elizabethan and Jacobean plays with such a setting were placed in Italy. Although *The Changeling* is set in Alicante, Spain, and the first major revenge tragedy of the period, Thomas Kyd's (?1557–94) *The Spanish Tragedy* (?1588), was also set in Spain, Elizabethans would have differentiated very little between the two places, and the background associations evoked in their minds would have been the same for those who had not visited either country. A series of intrigues and poisonings by the Borgia family and others in Italy conjured up an idea of a place where disputes were settled by a stab in the back, and not according to the supposedly English spirit of dealing in an open fashion. If there was no other way except physical confrontation, then an English gentleman should feel, like Alsemero in *The Changeling*, that satisfaction could be sought by means of a challenge to a duel – even though duelling itself was illegal and increasingly severe penalties were being invoked against it by James I's government at about the time when *The Changeling* was written. This would account for Beatrice's fear for Alsemero even if he were to win a duel against Alonzo (see II.2.24–39). *The Changeling* is set in a much less distinctly Italianate world than many other plays of the period. Intrigue and scheming are confined to Beatrice's machinations to avoid discovery and De Flores's assistance in this.

*Dorothy M. Farr, *Thomas Middleton and the Drama of Realism*, Oliver and Boyd, Edinburgh, 1973, p. 53.

Characters

The characters in *The Changeling* are essentially quite ordinary people, despite the fact that those in the main plot are from the upper ranks of society. The tragedy is domestic, and the fate of the characters is the direct result of their lack of foresight, their simplicity (wilful, uncontrollable desires are indeed simple), and in some cases their stupidity, as well as an absence of moral principles. The interest centres on the Beatrice-Joanna – De Flores relationship; after these two, the other characters are conventional figures.

A consideration of the characters in the subplot will be incorporated in the section entitled 'Subplot'.

Beatrice-Joanna

It is Beatrice, not De Flores, who precipitates the tragedy: the evil in him is released by her actions. Some critics have tended to romanticise her fall into sin, but Beatrice is no more a romantic heroine than Cressida in Shakespeare's *Troilus and Cressida*. She is no innocent, even at the start of the play, and therefore Middleton's own imagery which is suggestive of the Fall from Grace in the Garden of Eden is misplaced.*

Beatrice is by turns passionate, fickle, lustful, selfish, deceitful, stupid, cunning, ruthless, lacking in humanity, unimaginative, without judgment or self-awareness; yet as she is dying she attains a tragic and unsentimental assessment of herself. Her passion rules her, a passion which makes her the first and chief changeling in the play. Her change of affection from Alonzo to Alsemero is induced by lust, for there is no indication that she feels anything deeper for Alsemero. Later she is to show her fickleness by changing from loving Alsemero and loathing De Flores to deceiving the moral Alsemero and loving and admiring the evil De Flores. It is possible that her original irrational loathing for De Flores is an expression of a supressed lust for him, a lust which she subconsciously knows is explosively dangerous to her. De Flores himself is aware that the jump from hatred to loving is not a great one for an uncontrollably passionate nature, and it is this upon which he bases his initial hopes (see II.1.82–8). In the first three acts she behaves like a spoilt child, thinking that she must get just what she wants, and she has no feeling that others actually exist beyond their usefulness to her as objects of love or tools to use. In the final scene she talks to Alsemero of what she has done as a way 'to assure/Yourself to me' (V.3.70–71), as one might grab the best gown in a sale of clothes. Alonzo has been a thing to dispose of and De Flores one who would serve her purpose

*For a fuller examination of this theme in the play see David L. Frost's edition, Cambridge University Press, Cambridge, 1978, pp.413–14.

(II.2.69), so that she might have Alsemero and get 'rid ... Of two inveterate loathings at one time' (II.2.144–5). She thinks that she has been very clever (see III.4.13). It has often been objected that Beatrice could not have failed to see De Flores's motives in agreeing to carry out her murder; but her wilfulness and blind selfishness credibly override any such insight.

She never looks beyond the moment, and is easily lost in a situation (see III.4.72). She is an opportunist of the crudest kind, and never stops to think about the possible consequences of her actions or to weigh up the motives of others. When De Flores uses words like 'service', 'deed' or 'blood' she is unaware of possible innuendo – and this is the only sense in which she may be termed 'innocent'. She is quite lacking in self-awareness, and only gains some when it is already too late: 'Murder, I see, is followed by more sins' (III.4.164). Indeed, to her initial failings are now added adultery, trespassing, lying, bribery, procuring (this is what her ploy with Diaphanta amounts to), conspiracy and more murder. For Beatrice, as for Macbeth, crime becomes a habit; this for T. S. Eliot was the essence of the tragedy, and what makes it great.* If De Flores is the devil, she becomes the devil's creature.

However, the seeds of her ruthlessness were there earlier. She wished to have De Flores dismissed out of hand – 'discarded' is the word she uses, as if he were a piece of used paper (see II.1.92–3). Later on she is less confident in her ruthlessness:

> I must trust somebody.
>
> (V.1.15)

> I'm afraid now.
> This night hath been so tedious. Oh, this strumpet!
> Had she a thousand lives, he [De Flores] should not leave her
> Till he had destroyed the last. – List! Oh my terrors!
>
> (V.1.63–6)

She has become isolated from all normal humanity by her league with De Flores.

Her very success at avoiding detection by means of the virginity test suggests that she cannot hope to escape detection for ever. Neither her marriage nor her repeated fornication with De Flores has any future, but she never shows any awareness of this. Her assignations with De Flores are observed, and the end for her is near. Her lack of awareness is underlined when she is aghast at the sight of the severed finger, yet is without the imagination to grasp 'killing the whole man' (III.4.30). When she reacts to the murder of Alonzo as if she could escape the moral

*See *Elizabethan Dramatists*, Faber, London, 1963, pp. 85–6.

consequences of what she has done, it is De Flores who accurately reminds her what she now is:

> Push, you forget yourself!
> A woman dipp'd in blood, and talk of modesty!
>
> (III.4.125–6)

> Look but into your conscience, read me there.
> 'Tis a true book, you'll find me there your equal.
> Push! Fly not to your birth, but settle you
> In what the act has made you, y'are no more now;
> You must forget your parentage to me:
> Y'are the deed's creature; by that name
> You lost your first condition, and I challenge you,
> As peace and innocency has turn'd you out,
> And made you one with me.
>
> (III.4.132–40)

Crude awareness, of herself if of nobody else, comes in the crude line which suggests the violence of De Flores's love-making: 'this fellow has undone me endlessly' (IV.1.1). Implied also in this line is that she knows herself to be damned. Yet at the moment of her discovery by Alsemero at the end she still miscalculates, believing that the sin of murder will be understood, whereas the sin of adultery will not. Finally, the dying Beatrice starkly assesses the situation correctly in lines devoid of any sentimentality or self-pity (see V.3.149–61). Ironically, the wise platitudes which she speaks to Alsemero right at the begining of the play, little dreaming of applying them to herself, best sum up her predicament:

> Our eyes are sentinels unto our judgments,
> And should give certain judgment what they see;
> But they are rash sometimes and tell us wonders
> Of common things, which, when our judgments find,
> They then can check the eyes and call them blind
>
> (I.1.72–6)

Finally, despite all the criticism of her in this assessment of her character, it is vital to remember that we are presented with a human being; and that uppermost in the mind of the Jacobean spectator would have been not horror or judgment, but pity.

De Flores

At the beginning of the play De Flores is presented as a gentleman and follower of Vermandero whom Beatrice cannot stand the sight of, on account of his ugly face. For other people, De Flores is 'honest', 'kind and true', 'worth 'em all', 'kind De Flores', creating the same kind of public impression as Iago in Shakespeare's *Othello* (?1603)). It is only Tomazo's instinct, allied to the traditional belief that an ill-favoured face meant an ill-favoured mind, which leads him to regard De Flores as 'poison', as Beatrice did early in the play. Throughout, De Flores does nothing which is observably suspicious. He has very little about him of the familiar figure in Jacobean drama of the malcontent, although at first sight he may resemble him. A malcontent is so because of what he feels that society has done to him. De Flores is not aggrieved in this way; his behaviour springs entirely from within his own passions. His only complaint can be that he has been born ugly.

His main distinguishing feature is that he is intelligent, analytical and logical, where Beatrice is not. She later becomes a Machiavellian schemer, but he is one from the start. At no stage, however, does she match his efficiency and precision. Vermandero is right when he says that De Flores is 'good on all occasions' (V.1.90), whether it be in dealing with a fire or a dropped glove, or in countering Beatrice's horrified objections at the reward he proposes to claim for services rendered (see III.4.81–171). He assesses others correctly and he knows himself. His single-minded driving lust for Beatrice does not lead him to lose his judgment, as Beatrice loses hers. What he does may be careless of the future, but he knows what he is doing, realising that love/lust is 'beyond all reason' (II.1.84). Near ecstacy, he is nonetheless not taken in by Beatrice's artfulness as she sets about seducing him to the murder:

> 'Tis the same physnomy, to a hair and pimple
> Which she call'd scurvy scarce an hour ago;
> How is this?
>
> (II.2.76–8)

The murder of Alonzo is nothing to him if it promises to satisfy his desires:

> . . . for the deed,
> I feel no weight in't, 'tis but light and cheap
> For the sweet recompense that I set down for't.
>
> (III.4.18–20)

As in some species of animal, the drive to couple sexually is his main aim in life. It does not matter to him that there is no future beyond the immediate in his relationship with Beatrice. His awareness of this allows him to be quite open when confronted with his crimes (see V.3.104–5, 162–3), freely acknowledging the nature of the evil he has committed (unlike Beatrice, who admits the worst of her crimes, largely because she thinks that in the circumstances murder is the more socially acceptable one to which to confess). Even the recurring appearance of Alonzo's ghost does not seem to disturb him unduly, for he knows that he is damned. When the end comes, he is as resigned to it as Edmund in *King Lear* or Iago in *Othello*:

> I lov'd this woman in spite of her heart;
> Her love I earn'd out of Piracquo's murder . . . .
> Yes, and her honour's prize
> Was my reward; I thank life for nothing
> But that pleasure; it was so sweet to me
> That I have drunk up all, left none behind
> For any man to pledge me.

(V.3.165–71)

Whatever else he may be, De Flores is no changeling.

Alsemero

Alsemero is important in the play on account of what he stands for, and it sometimes seems that Middleton is only interested in him insofar as he affects Beatrice's actions. He is given no lines of any wit or humour which might have made his personality more attractive. Despite Beatrice's platitudes about eyes and judgment, it can only be his outside with which she falls in love.

At the beginning of the play Alsemero is as much a changeling as any: he changes from a traveller who spurns any thought of settling down to woo a woman, to a love-lorn waverer (see I.1.52–4) who is prepared to give up the pursuit of Beatrice rather easily (see I.1.199–201). However, he is quickly established after this as a moral gentleman. He is prepared to win Beatrice by fighting a duel which, while legally dubious, is at least in accord with a conventional code of honour (see II.2.27–8). Soon after this Beatrice and De Flores take the centre of the stage, and we do not see a great deal of Alsemero. Nonetheless, during this time he implicitly becomes the representative of reality, normality and morality and Beatrice has to work hard to outmanoeuvre him. In trying to secure him she has made him her moral enemy. She fears his perception and his judgment; he is

> One who's ennobled both in blood and mind,
> So clear in understanding (that's my plague now),
> Before whose judgment will my fault appear
> Like malefactors' crimes before tribunals;
> There is no hiding on't . . .

(IV.1.5–9)

His judgment is unclouded, unlike that of Alonzo. He can reason, and hence is capable of scepticism; he keeps an open mind when Beatrice is observed departing from De Flores in suspicious circumstances. He is the equal and opposite of De Flores in the play: he is his equal in reasoning and the sexual attraction Beatrice finds in him; he is his opposite in his morality. Between the two stands the amoral Beatrice herself.

The final scene of the play belongs to Alsemero, as the moral order is restored. If he has wavered at the beginning, his efficiency and moral decisiveness in dealing with the guilty pair when he confronts them is as impressive as De Flores's energy. Alsemero is ruthless in his judgment of them (see V.3.114–42, where he sweeps all before him in his domination of the action). After the deaths of Beatrice and De Flores he comments on the other characters, assesses the nature of justice in the play, and sums up its moral, finally holding the stage for the epilogue.

Vermandero

Vermandero is the governor of the castle at Alicante, and is clearly a powerful man. Throughout the play he behaves with a combination of dignity and haughtiness which suggests that he is one who is not used to being crossed. This is established in the first scene of the play when he speaks of the intended marriage between Alonzo and his daughter: 'He shall be bound to me,/As fast as this tie can hold him; I'll want/My will else'; to which Beatrice reacts: 'I shall want mine if you do it' (I.1.219–21). Vermandero talks here not only in terms of his complete control over his daughter, which would have been seen as quite acceptable by the Jacobean audience; but he behaves as if Alonzo had no right to a mind of his own. This, together with Beatrice's rebellious reply aside, suggests that he has for a daughter the spoilt, wilful child that he deserves. If you look through the play you will see occasions when he uses 'we', 'our' and 'us' almost as if he saw himself as a royal personage. Examine his various appearances in the play to see whether you can find evidence to support or refute the view of Vermandero given here.

Diaphanta

In the first scene Diaphanta displays a willingness to be drawn into bawdy conversation with Jasperino (I.1.137–53). Later, she comments to Beatrice on the anticipated delights of the marriage bed, and is quick to take up the opportunity of replacing Beatrice therein. These factors may well lead us to share Beatrice's doubts as to whether Diaphanta is still a maid. The virginity test, in which we must believe, demonstrates that she is still intact; but virgin or not, her libidinous nature is already established before her uncontrollable lust leads her to linger in Alsemero's bed.

The significance of Diaphanta is the parallel between her nature and that of Beatrice. The only difference between them is that between appearance and reality. Diaphanta is patently lustful, Beatrice hides her lustfulness under a mask of modesty, the kind of mask that is recognised for what it is and torn aside by Alsemero at the end (see V.3.46–8). As with her mistress, the inability to control her nature costs this changeling-in-the-marriage-bed her life.

Alonzo de Piracquo

Alonzo is an ordinary, unimaginative man. He is well-meaning, and the fact that there is nothing of the sceptic about him leads to his downfall. He judges superficially, and when his brother observes Beatrice's behaviour and then raises reasonable doubt as to her love for Alonzo, he reacts in a conventionally gallant but essentially stupid way (see II.1.123–55). He spurns Tomazo like a potential enemy, and cannot see that only the closest of friends would point out to him that in this matter he may be making a mistake. In his own way, he is as self-willed as Beatrice, refusing to recognise any obstacle to his desires. Tomazo, who is one of the characters in the play whose judgment is unclouded (Alsemero, Jasperino, Lollio and Isabella are the others), can well see that Alonzo's blindness is a result of 'love's tame madness' by which means 'a man/Quickly steals into his vexation' (II.1.154–5). In his guilelessness Alonzo is no match for the Italianate assassin De Flores.

Tomazo de Piracquo

Tomazo is a conventional revenger in embryo; but he is never allowed to develop, as this is not a play which is principally interested in revenge. In IV.2. and V.2 he shows the typical revenger's melancholy and misanthropy, but his scenes are short, and he himself acknowledges that he does not have a single clue to work upon. He is in no way in the centre of affairs, like Hamlet is in Shakespeare's *Hamlet* or Vindice in Tourneur's *The Revenger's Tragedy* (?1606), and in his floundering to discover the identity of the murderer he ironically appeals to the murderer himself. Dorothy Farr comments that Tomazo's 'interest is in retribution rather than revenge . . . Tomazo has no concern with revenge in the conventional sense; he is content if justice is done and shows no desire to be its instrument'.* This is not altogether true, for at the moment when he believes that the murderers are to be placed at his mercy he shows more than a trace of personal vindictiveness: 'I thirst for'em;/Like subtle lightning will I wind about 'em,/And melt their

***Thomas Middleton and The Drama of Realism*, Oliver and Boyd, Edinburgh, 1973, p. 64.

marrow in 'em' (V.2.85–7). However at the end, when the two criminals have destroyed one another without the intervention of a human revenger, he has the 'peace' that he sought (see V.2.83), and considers that the vengeance of hell is wreaking more than his anger ever could. He does not feel in any way thwarted because the guilty pair have escaped him by taking their own lives:

> . . . I am satisfied; my injuries
> Lie dead before me. I can exact no more,
> Unless my soul were loose, and could o'ertake
> Those black fugitives that are fled from thence,
> To take a second vengeance; but there are wraths
> Deeper than mine, 'tis to be fear'd, about 'em.
>
> (V.3.190–95)

The subplot

In the seventeenth century, *The Changeling* was famous, not for the psychological intensity of its main plot, but for the comic subplot. Antonio was one of the most popular of all stage characters. About half the length of the main plot, the subplot is an ironic burlesque commentary on the main action. The two are interwoven thematically and structurally, and the Jacobean audience would have seen nothing strange in the intermingling of tragedy and farce; tragi-comedies were common.

However, nearer our own day, critical taste has often found the subplot scarcely satisfying. R. H. Barker felt that 'It would be nice . . . if we could forget that the play has a comic story at all',* Una Ellis-Fermor considered that the subplot could indeed be omitted with no damage to the main story;† Algernon Swinburne called 'the underplot . . . very stupid, rather coarse, and almost vulgar.'‡ *Almost* vulgar? It certainly *is* vulgar, and properly so, for it parodies that which is masked by decorum in the main plot. The subplot deals openly with the crude sexuality which is just beneath the surface in the main action, and its repeated use of bawdy puns and innuendos sharpens our ears to the significance of double meanings present in the play's more intense moments. A more reasonable accusation against the subplot is not that it is irrelevant, but that, apart from the *double-entendres* and the antic clowning of Antonio and Franciscus, it is dull. Seeing a good production of the play will show you that in performance it can be anything but dull.

***Thomas Middleton*, Columbia University Press, New York, 1958, p. 129.

†See her *The Jacobean Drama*, Methuen, London, 1936, p. 144.

‡See his Introduction to the original Mermaid edition of Middleton's plays, T. Fisher Unwin, London, 1887, p. xxxv.

The thematic links between the two plots cannot be denied: the madness of love; the difference between appearance and reality, mental blindness and insight; the transformation or 'changing' of characters. As Alonzo displays 'love's madness', so Antonio and Franciscus change themselves in order to pursue the madness of love in a madhouse. We see the farcical effects of mad infatuation highlighted, and become the more aware of what is happening to the characters in the main action. In several ways – which you will find worth exploring in greater detail – Isabella, Lollio, Alibius and Antonio/Franciscus are distorted reflections of Beatrice, De Flores, Alonzo and Alsemero. Isabella is tempted to become a 'whore in her affection' and be untrue to her husband, Alibius, by Antonio and Franciscus, with Lollio watching eagerly for her fall; Beatrice is tempted to cut herself free from her betrothed, Alonzo, in order to be available for Alsemero, while De Flores is eager to seize the opportunity to – in Lollio's words – 'put in for his thirds'. Isabella maintains her judgment and sees how things are, preserving the moral order; Beatrice loses control and descends into disorder and chaos. Alibius's function is to attempt to cure mental madness, and Isabella's is to cure sexual madness. She succeeds in bringing Antonio to an awareness of his folly. 'A woman . . .', says Lollio, 'has an eye more than a man' (III.3.79–80); setting aside for the moment the sexual innuendo, Lollio's comment is true of Isabella, but not of Beatrice. Isabella is no changeling; unlike Beatrice. It is a macabre masterstroke of the theatre to display the folly of the main plot against the background of lunacy. Ironically, it is the good sense of Isabella in the confinement of the madhouse which offers an escape from madness to be found in the main action only through a tragic ending; and even then, the escape of Beatrice and De Flores is via death to the confinement of hell.

There are many verbal echoes of the main plot in the subplot. Beatrice, when confused, is lost 'in a labyrinth' (III.4.72) which leads to her ruin; Isabella, in her pretended madness, says 'let us tread the lower labyrinth;/I'll bring thee to the clue' (IV.3.111–2) – she has a 'clue' to the way out of the maze. De Flores declares 'His end's upon him' (II.2.135) when he learns from Beatrice who it is that he must kill in order to serve her; when Franciscus learns that in order to win Isabella's love he must confront his rival, he cries 'He's dead already!' (IV.3.201). Lollio and De Flores are both described by various other characters as 'honest'. You should search through the play for more examples.

Whatever opinion you may hold about the success or otherwise of the subplot, the old story of an aging husband who struggles to prevent younger men from seducing his young wife and cuckolding him has a stage history going back to Roman comedy and beyond, and is invariably enjoyed by audiences. It is clear that the playwrights intended the subplot to be unified with the main plot, and at the end of the play this connection is made plain. Isabella warns Alibius that he must be a changeling, and transform himself from a jealous husband to one who sees clearly the value of his wife. Alibius replies that he sees 'all apparent, wife, and will change now/Into a better husband' (V.3.213–14).

For a full discussion of the subplot see pp. lxii-lxviii of N. W. Bawcutt's Revels edition of the play, Methuen, London, 1958.

Comic elements in the main plot

Before Middleton wrote *The Changeling* he was principally a writer of comedies which were concerned with the domestic and other problems of ordinary London citizens. This kind of play has become known as 'citizen comedy'. An examination of *The Changeling* shows that he used many of the techniques of comedy in order to give shape to elements in the main plot which eventually lead to tragedy. An example of this is the presentation of De Flores, who in some respects is the type of downtrodden servant wanting to find favour with a beautiful lady, which a contemporary audience would have recognised as a potential figure of fun. This expectation, tempered early on by comments from De Flores such as 'Though I get nothing else, I'll have my will' (I.1.238), combine to create an uneasy world in which we are not sure what is comedy and what is tragedy.

The following exchange between Beatrice and De Flores, when she is trying, in a not very subtle way, to manipulate him so that he will 'serve her turn', has considerable comic potential:

BEATRICE: . . . – Oh, my De Flores!
DE FLORES: (*aside*) How's that? She calls me hers already, 'my De Flores'!
– You were about to sigh out somewhat, madam?
BEATRICE: No, was I? I forgot. – Oh!
DE FLORES: There 'tis again,
The very fellow on't.
BEATRICE: You are too quick, sir.
DE FLORES: There's no excuse for't now; I heard it twice, madam;
That sigh would fain have utterance, take pity on't,
And lend it a free word; 'las, how it labours
For liberty! I hear the murmur yet
Beat at your bosom.
BEATRICE: Would creation –
DE FLORES: Ay, well said, that's it.
BEATRICE: Had form'd me man!
DE FLORES: Nay, that's not it.

(II.2.98–109)

As this scene goes on, there is a certain comic irony in the way that both characters become increasingly excited at the prospect of the fulfilment of their desires – and in the fact that they mistakenly think they understand one another:

BEATRICE: . . . Thy reward shall be precious.
DE FLORES: That I have thought on;
I have assur'd myself of that beforehand.
And I know it will be precious; the thought ravishes.
BEATRICE: Then take him to thy fury!
DE FLORES: I thirst for him.
BEATRICE: Alonzo de Piracquo!
DE FLORES: His end's upon him: he shall be seen no more.
BEATRICE: How lovely now dost thou appear to me!
Never was man dearlier rewarded.
DE FLORES: I do think of that.

(II.2.129–38)

De Flores's cutting off of the dead Alonzo's finger may not be thought funny, but in the theatre audiences invariably both gasp and laugh as De Flores struggles to get the ring off the finger:

What, so fast on?
Not part in death? I'll take the speedy course then,
Finger and all shall off.
(*Cuts off the finger*)

(III.2.23–5)

A grim humour is also generated later when he presents the finger with the ring still on it to Beatrice:

DE FLORES: I've a token for you.
BEATRICE: For me?
DE FLORES: But it was sent somewhat unwillingly;
I could not get the ring without the finger.
(*He shows the finger*)
BEATRICE: Bless me! What hast thou done?

(III.4.26–9)

The mere mention of 'finger' was often taken as an obscene pun for 'penis' and the humorous symbolism of the physical presentation to Beatrice of a finger with a ring on it would not have been lost on the Jacobean audience. Later in this scene, Beatrice's moral indignation and 'honourable' outrage when she realises that De Flores wants sexual surrender from her are almost amusing, and the audience would certainly endorse De Flores's reminder to her of the kind of woman she has now become (see III.4.120–6). The whole business of the virginity test borders on the absurd, but Middleton had good dramatic sense and the episodes generate in an audience a mixture of amusement and fascination as they wait to see how Beatrice will deal with her problems. Diaphanta's eagerness to lose her virginity is reminiscent of those country innocents in Jacobean citizen comedy who arrive in town eager for pleasure (see IV.1), and her apology to Beatrice at being unable to tear herself away from Alsemero's bed could have come straight from a comedy – 'In troth I was so well, I ev'n forgot myself' (V.1.78). De Flores's brisk efficiency as he sets about saving the situation in V.1. has a distinctly humorous, albeit macabre, character. We know that the aim of all this rumpus is to winkle Diaphanta out of Alsemero's bed and to murder her, but the humour is derived from Vermandero's approval as De Flores, who started the fire, sets about extinguishing it:

VERMANDERO: Oh bless my house and me!
ALSEMERO: My lord your father.
Enter DE FLORES *with a piece.*
VERMANDERO: Knave, whither goes that piece?
DE FLORES: To scour the chimney. *Exit.*
VERMANDERO: Oh, well said, well said;
That fellow's good on all occasions.
BEATRICE: A wondrous necessary man, my lord.
VERMANDERO: He hath a ready wit, he's worth 'em all, sir;
Dog at a house of fire; I ha' seen him sing'd ere now.
The piece goes off,
Ha, there he goes.
BEATRICE: 'Tis done.

(V.1.87–94)

Vermandero's ignorance of what is really going on creates ironic comedy, which is made the more effective by the chilling two words from Beatrice, not understood by the others, underlining for us what the thing is that has in fact been done – murder. As this scene progresses, and the ignorant offer De Flores rewards for what is in fact villainy, it is difficult for us not to share in his delight. Similar responses are generated in audiences watching and listening to Edmund in *King Lear* or Gloucester in *Richard III*. And when Alsemero confronts De Flores with the truth, he does not try to evade the fact that the game is up, but acknowledges his guilt with a wry joke:

ALSEMERO: My wife's behindhand with you, she tells me,
For a brave bloody blow you gave for her sake
Upon Piracquo.
DE FLORES: Upon? 'Twas quite through him, sure.

(V.3.102–4)

It can thus be seen that the moments of potential or actual comedy in the main plot in no way detract from the tragedy; if anything, they help to throw into relief this powerful tragedy of human deception and self-deception. Through the play runs the image of the old game of barley-brake, played by ordinary folk and incorporating elements of fun, sex and hell; it is this metaphor, uniting laughter and hell-fire, with which De Flores leaves us at the end of the play: 'Yes, and the while I coupled with your mate/At barley-brake; now we are left in Hell' (V.3.162–3). Comedy and tragedy come together in a game.

Imagery

What is an image?

This question perplexes many students. They should be comforted to know that eminent critics disagree among themselves as to the answer. The following are the two main schools of thought:
(a) An image is a use of language which stimulates a *visual* image in the mind of the reader or listener.
(b) An image is a use of language which stimulates in the mind an impression of *any* of the five senses, that is, touch, sound, smell and taste, as well as sight.

As to what particular use of language may evoke an image, critics are also divided. Here, there are again two main schools of thought, as follows:
(a) An image can be created only by figurative language, that is, similes or metaphor.
(b) An image can be created by an effective direct description which is not necessarily a simile or a metaphor.

The definitions preferred by the author of these Notes are both those indicated as (b) above. (For amplification of the above distinctions there is a good chapter entitled 'Imagery' in Patrick Murray's *Literary Criticism: a glossary of major terms*, Longman, London, 1978).

Where drama is concerned, a potential image can be present in the words, which can only be fully realised in production, e.g. the set design and stage effects for, say, III, 3 of *The Changeling* may be chosen in order to give a framework for the verbal imagery of Isabella's confinement. Stage directors sometimes call these possibilities by the name of 'sub-text'.

Imagery in *The Changeling*

In this section there follow a few general comments on the nature of the imagery in *The Changeling*. Then, instead of all the work being done for you in the form of a commentary under separate headings for each distinctive kind of imagery, there will be a long list of line references to images in order of appearance in the play. It is very far from a complete list, and you will find many others. However, you should look up all the references and list the images under appropriate headings, adding any others which you notice and which you find striking.

Images of MADNESS, LOVE/LUST and CHANGEABLENESS, verbal and visual, abound in both main plot and the subplot, as do images of IMPRISONMENT (Alsemero locks Beatrice and De Flores in his closet), CONFINEMENT (Alibius will not let Isabella leave the house) and CLAUSTROPHOBIA (Vermandero's castle). There are many metaphors related to SIGHT and BLINDNESS in the play. There are images with RELIGIOUS overtones, related to the serpent De Flores and Beatrice's Fall from Grace into Sin. Images of FOOD are contrasted with those of POISON. The BODY features prominently (the dead man's finger in III.2 and III.4 brings home to Beatrice the reality of the murder, and suggests the crudeness of De Flores' sexual drive towards her). The CUCKOO is a metaphor for cuckoldry. BLOOD is frequently mentioned (De Flores sees Beatrice as dipped in it, and she later sees herself as a bad part of her father's blood, to be let out for his better HEALTH, images of which are balanced in the play by those of SICKNESS. LIGHT symbolises 'clear understanding'. The day star heralds the dawn, and Beatrice is a guilty thing that has reason to fear its coming; Alonzo's ghost passes in front of the light of the star, extinguishing it momentarily. The star also suggests FIRE: lust will burn De Flores's heart to cinders, and he starts a fire which he claims has consumed the lustful Diaphanta.

The Changeling is not a play notable for its imagery. What is there tends to stand out, underlining the difference between what is normal and accepted and what is abnormal or frightening. Look up the following references, and see how they fit in with what is written above:

ACT I

I.1.24–5, 72–9, 84, 93, 107, 109, 121–7, 137–53, 190, 208.
I.2.70, 215–16, 228–33.

ACT II

II.1.15–19, 45, 50–51, 55, 79, 95, 151, 154.
II.2.18, 24–30, 46–7, 80–90, 111–13, 116–24, 132, 145–56.

ACT III

III.2.8–9. 12–14, 25.
III.3.44–5, 60, 66–7, 77–92, 124, 171–2, 179–83, 189–204, 257–89.
III.4.18, 26–45, 71, 107, 126–31, 151–3, 162–3.

ACT IV

IV.1.s.d., 5–6, 104–6, 128.
IV.2.64–7, 103–4, 106, 144, 150.
IV.3.75–85, 111, 125–56, 167–78.

ACT V
V.1.2–7, 25, 31–7, 56, 58–9, 68–73, 84–5, 93, 106–8, 115–16.
V.2.15–19, 31–3, 85–7.
V.3.7–9, 14–18, 32–5, 46–7, 50–4, 56, 65–7, 74–7, 81, 85–7, 95–9, 103, 109, 127–9, 135, 147–57, 162–5, 169–71, 196–219.

Irony

Irony is a term used to describe words which are charged with a layer of meaning different from the literal one; the subtler interpretation of which the hearer may or may not be aware. The least subtle form of irony is blatant sarcasm. More specifically, dramatic irony is a term used to describe a situation in which the speaker is unaware of the significance of what he is saying. The audience, however, is or will soon become aware of the irony. In comedy, this gives rise to mirth; in tragedy, to pain.

If you turn to Part 4 of these Notes, you will find a specimen answer on irony in *The Changeling* (Question 16).

Revenge

Background

During the Middle Ages, and then during the Tudor period (1485–1603), a legal system was gradually constructed which provided a formal way of dealing with murder. It came to be accepted that vengeance taken by an individual was wrong, and symptomatic of a chaotic, anarchic society, and that if a revenge was to be taken, then society would do it – and would call it not revenge, but justice. If society failed to bring the criminal to justice for any reason, then it was considered right that any individual who wished to see the offender punished should not take the law into his own hands, but should leave the said offender to God's justice (see the Bible, 'Vengeance is mine; I will repay, saith the lord', Romans 12:19). This attitude also applied to duelling: it may have been considered an honourable way for a gentleman to confront one who had wronged him, but by Elizabethan times it was increasingly considered to be another way of taking the law into one's own hands, and as reprehensible as taking revenge by means of a stab in the back or poison. The most concise statement on revenge in the time of Thomas Middleton is Sir Francis Bacon's essay *Of Revenge* (1612). As well as being a philosopher, statesman, scientist and writer, Bacon was also a lawyer, having served at one time and another as Solicitor General and Attorney General, and so his essay may be said to be a valid reflection of both the moral and legal standpoints of the time:

> Revenge is a kind of wild justice; which the more a man's nature runs to, the more ought law to weed it out. For as for the first wrong, it doth but offend the law; but the revenge of that wrong putteth the law out of office. Certainly, in taking revenge, a man is but even with his enemy; but in passing it over, he is superior; for it is a prince's part to pardon. And Solomon, I am sure, saith: 'It is the glory of a man to pass by an offence.' That which is past is gone, and irrevocable; and wise men have enough to do with things present and to come: therefore they do but trifle with themselves, that labour in past matters .... The most tolerable sort of revenge is for those wrongs which there is no law to remedy; but then let a man take heed the revenge be such, as there is no law to punish .... Some, when they take revenge, are desirous the party should know whence it cometh: this is the more generous. For the delight seemeth to be not so much in doing the hurt as in making the party repent: but base and crafty cowards are like the arrow that flieth in the dark .... This is certain, that a man that studieth revenge keeps his own wounds green, which otherwise would heal and do well....

Revenge plays

The earliest revenge plays of the Elizabethan period tended to be translations or imitations of the Roman plays of Seneca (*d.*AD65), the philosopher and dramatist. They were by and large devoid of subtlety of characterisation, plot or language, relying on startling coincidences and ultimate violence and bloodshed for their effect. *Gorboduc* is a good example of an early revenge play. *The Spanish Tragedy* by Thomas Kyd set the pattern for revenge plays for some time, being the most popular tragedy of the 1590s. Its formula became almost a blueprint for succeeding revenge tragedies; a ghost appears who wishes to see vengeance exacted on his behalf; the main character, Hieronimo, seeks legal redress for the murder of his son but, failing to find it, vows personal vengeance; his subsequent behaviour ranges from melancholy malcontentedness to madness; he contemplates suicide; his drive for revenge corrupts his character; eventually he gains his revenge, killing his enemies but dying himself. Shakespeare's *Hamlet* (?1601) contains similar motifs, and marks the beginning of a period during which some very powerful revenge plays were written, such as Chapman's *Bussy D'Ambois* (?1604), Tourneur's *The Revenger's Tragedy* (?1607), Webster's *The White Devil* and *The Duchess of Malfi* and Middleton's *Women Beware Women* (?1621).

The occasional play appeared, for example Tourneur's *The Athiest's Tragedy* (?1611), in which the hero, sometimes after hesitation, leaves revenge to heaven: whereupon heaven obliges, and the potential revenger survives. A curious variation on the theme is *A Woman Killed With Kindness* (1603) by Thomas Heywood (*c*.1573–1641), where Frankford treats his erring wife with such forbearance and Christian 'kindness' that she, riddled with remorse, pines away and dies. The last good play of the period which contains a strong revenge motif is Ford's *'Tis Pity She's a Whore.*

Revenge and justice in *The Changeling*

Several features which are typical of a revenge play are present in the final scene of *The Changeling*: the doomed villain's unrepentant satisfaction with what he has accomplished, a corrupted person's wish to be allowed to sink into oblivion (see V.3.150–3, and compare the Cardinal's words in the final scene of Webster's *The Duchess of Malfi*, V.5.88–9), the violent deaths. Earlier, Alsemero considers challenging Alonzo to a duel, although Alonzo can hardly be said to have 'wronged' him, except insofar as he is a rival who is to marry Beatrice against her will; the situation is never developed. There are also vestiges of the revenge genre in the melancholy discontent of Tomazo and in the appearances of Alonzo's ghost.

However, *The Changeling* is not a conventional revenge play, and the focus of attention is the development of the Beatrice – De Flores relationship. It is not human revenge which is seen, but the inexorable operation of divine justice and retribution. The title of Middleton's main source for the plot may give us this clue: *The Triumphs of God's Revenge against ... Murder* (1621) by John Reynolds. It is Beatrice herself who recognises this when, trapped by De Flores, she says 'Vengeance begins ...' (III.4.164); in the context she can only be referring to divine Vengeance/Justice for what she has done. At the end of the play, after De Flores and Beatrice are dead, Alsemero turns to Tomazo and says: 'Sir, you are sensible of what truth hath done;/'Tis the best comfort that your grief can find' (V.3.188–9). He might almost have read Bacon's essay.

In relation to this topic you should examine closely the whole of the final scene of the play. See also the note on Tomazo on pp. 60–1.

Verse

Middleton's verse in *The Changeling* is unremarkable in itself; but as dramatic verse it is effective. It is straightforward, economic, bare in style, almost the exact opposite of the dazzling imagery of Middleton's contemporary, John Webster. A good example of Middleton's style in this play can be seen in the following speech by Beatrice, where she realises that De Flores intends sexual blackmail:

Why, 'tis impossible thou canst be so wicked,
Or shelter such a cunning cruelty,
To make his death the murderer of my honour!
Thy language is so bold and vicious,
I cannot see which way I can forgive it
With any modesty.

(III.4.120–5)

Apart from the personification of death in line 122, the verse is matter-of-fact and colourless. The evidence of his other plays shows that Middleton is capable of writing with much greater vividness, and it is clear that he is here, and throughout *The Changeling*, putting the development of situation, plot and character first. He is using verse as a skilled director might use subtle lighting effects in the theatre or background music in a film – they are frequently the more effective for being unobstrusive.

However, there are lines in the play which stand on their own and live on in the mind of the hearer. In response to the speech quoted above, De Flores scoffs: 'A woman dipp'd in blood, and talk of modesty!' (III.4.126); and later in the same scene, when Beatrice goes down on her knees to him, weeping for mercy, he ends her appeals by saying to her: 'Can you weep Fate from its determin'd purpose?/So soon may you weep me' (III.4.162–3). Beatrice's dying speech (V.3.149–61) is unusual in the sustained strength of its imagery, quite unlike any other passage in the play.

Go through the play and see what other examples you can find of (a) matter-of-fact, rather colourless verse which is nonetheless effective in its context, (b) more immediately exciting poetry, such as the lines from De Flores's and Beatrice's speeches to which reference has just been made.

Performance history

The Changeling was very popular in Jacobean times, and the fact that it was first printed during the period of the Commonwealth suggests that it even found favour with the Puritans who were usually against any notion of stage plays. Perhaps the clear moral implications of the inevitable ruin which is brought on by sin appealed to them. When the Puritan era ended and the Monarchy was restored the play continued to be performed, first by a newly formed company at the Phoenix Theatre where the celebrated actor Thomas Betterton (?1635–1710) played De Flores, apparently to great applause. There is a record of a performance of the play during the Restoration period at an inn called the Cardinal's Cap, situated near Pembroke Hall, Cambridge, and in his diaries

Samuel Pepys (1633–1703) notes down how he went 'by water to Whitefriars to the Playhouse and there saw *The Changeling*, the first time it has been acted these twenty years, and it takes exceedingly'.

During the eighteenth, nineteenth and early part of the twentieth century the play was out of favour, although some adaptations were made and performed with very limited success. The first modern revival seems to have been by the First Folio Theatre Club at the Interval Theatre Club on 3 May 1950. On 20 November 1950 BBC Radio broadcast a version with the subplot left out. There was one performance staged at Wyndham's Theatre, London, on 16 May 1954. The Experimental Theatre Club performed the play in Oxford in November 1956. A production of the play ran for a month at the Royal Court Theatre, London, in the Spring of 1961, with Robert Shaw as De Flores and Mary Ure as Beatrice. There was a student production by the Lady Margaret Players at St John's College, Cambridge, in January 1964, and another in March 1965 by Durham University Theatre (in which the author of these Notes played Alibius). *The Changeling* was performed by the Lyceum Company at the Edinburgh Festival in 1970. The most recent major production was the BBC television version which was broadcast on 20 January 1974, with Helen Mirren as Beatrice and Stanley Baker as De Flores.

Part 4

Hints for study

Preparing for the examination

In preparing for the examination you have probably read the play more than once; gone through it at least once in close detail, sometimes spending a whole session on the language, tone, character revelation and suchlike points of interest embodied in a single speech; and also, it is to be hoped, you have seen a performance of the play. The last is not always easy since performances of a set play, other than Shakespeare, are rarely available when you want them. If you are lucky, however, and hear of a production of *The Changeling*, even one for which you have to travel a distance, it is worth making the effort to see it. Even if it turns out to be an interpretation of the play which you think is wrong – perhaps particularly if this is the case – it is valuable because you are driven back to reviewing the text and testing your view of the play against that of the director and cast of the production you have seen. Also, you have been reminded that what you are studying is a piece of drama and not a book; and that its verse is dramatic verse, intended to be heard rather than read.

As the day of the examination draws closer, you will want to find ways of bringing your knowledge and understanding of the text to a peak, without driving out all freshness of response so that there is no enjoyment left in it for you. If this happens there is a danger that your essays in the examination will be dull and mechanical.

Monotony can best be avoided by setting yourself varied tasks. Here are some suggestions:

(*a*) Spend some time reading through the entire play again, writing a series of symbols in the margin denoting different aspects of interest. For instance, you might write 'C' against words which illuminate facets of a character, either of the speaker or of another; 'I' could be written in the margin alongside a distinctive piece of imagery; 'T' adjacent to a notable theme which runs through the play; 'IR' for irony; and so on, inventing other symbols for any recurrent aspects of the play which you notice. When you have finished the play, make a list of references under different headings: this will help you to assemble your own thoughts and develop your own opinions.

(*b*) Commit to memory some useful *short* quotations – words, phrases, a few lines at most in each instance. You will find some useful ones used under various headings in Part 3 of these Notes.
(*c*) Write a paragraph summarising each act. Then try to summarise each act in two or three sentences. By comparing the two versions you can tell things about the dramatic structure. Which elements are vital? What have you left out in your second version and why? How much has the plot lost by your omissions?
(*d*) Ask somebody to start reading at random from the play: see how quickly you can identify the quotation, saying as much as you can about its context.
(*e*) Athletes train over the distance which they are going to run in competition: so should examinees. The examination will require you to answer a number of questions in a given time, and it is vital that you have accustomed yourself to this pressure. Find out how long you will have to write each essay in the examination. Then sit down in a quiet place, choose a title for a test essay, and do whatever reading and note-taking you think necessary by way of preparation. When you are ready, put all books and notes away, get out pen and paper, set an alarm clock for ten minutes less than your allotted time, and commence writing your essay (see (5) below under the heading *In the examination*). When the alarm rings, you have five minutes to draw the essay to a conclusion, and five minutes to check it through for mistakes. Leave the essay and come back to it later. How does it read? Did you say what you meant to? Did you leave out anything? Did you include anything which now seems irrelevant and better left out? Ask a teacher or lecturer to assess your essay if you can.

After a couple of attempts at this exercise, you may feel confident enough to write two essays consecutively. There is no point in the exercise unless you create examination room conditions for yourself. Write entirely uninterrupted: no background music and no getting up to make a cup of coffee in the middle.

In the examination

Here are some suggestions to help you in the examination room. They are numbered in order to give you a rough idea as to the sequence in which they may be considered:

(1) If there is a choice of question, consider carefully which will suit you best; but do not take too long to decide. Check how many questions you are required to answer on the paper as a whole.
(2) Read carefully your chosen question. If there are key words which

you feel need clarifying, do that in the opening paragraph of your answer.

(3) If a question is in two parts, divide your time equally between each part, unless you can show in your answer why one aspect is more important than another.

(4) Answer the question asked. However good your ideas, they are worthless if misapplied. An art examiner was once asked, if a candidate is asked to paint an oak tree and he paints instead a perfect cedar tree, what the painting is worth. The reply was 'Nothing'.

(5) Jot down a skeleton answer outlining the subject matter of each paragraph before you start to write the essay. As you write you may well find that new ideas emerge: be flexible and allow for these, departing from your plan if necessary. But if you start with no plan, then your essay will have no direction at any stage of its writing.

(6) Write legibly. An examiner probably has several hundred scripts to read: he will not be so well disposed towards a script which is very difficult to decipher.

(7) Keep your style clear and direct. Only use literary jargon when strictly appropriate; avoid impressive-sounding but long-winded and empty phraseology.

(8) Unless the question specifies an account, avoid narrative; use it only when necessary to illustrate your argument. Merely to tell the story as an answer to most questions is virtually worthless.

(9) Do not quote long passages. It is rare to find that more than two or three lines are relevant to any particular point, and it is painfully obvious to an examiner when a candidate has learnt a passage and is determined to fit it into his answer, whether or not it is pertinent to the argument in hand. ('Quotation' is the noun – not 'Quote', which is the verb.)

(10) There is no need to cite precise references. They are included in these Notes in order to help you to follow up and expand upon ideas. Wherever you can, indicate the Act and Scene of a reference or quotation; it will hardly be expected that you should have line references at your command.

(11) Refer to *The Changeling* as 'the play' – never 'the book'.

(12) Never refer to a character as an 'actor' While you should remember that you are dealing with a play, the term 'actor' refers to one who is playing the character, and not to the character him/herself.

(13) Only use a concluding paragraph if you have something more to say. You may wish to tie up some loose ends, or to assert a conclusion which you feel has not been sufficiently stressed; but it is a waste of time merely to repeat in summary what you have already said at length.

(14) Try to leave time to read through your answer, particularly if you know you are prone to make careless slips.

(15) The examination has a time limit. You should have worked out at the beginning how long you have for each question. Keep to your schedule as closely as possible. It helps if you are ruthless over omitting unnecessary information, however tempted you may be to demonstrate to the examiner the range of your knowledge. If you do run short of time, resort to note form: display as much of your argument as possible, showing how the essay would have developed.

Questions

In the study of literature there is no such thing as a correct answer. Questions are asked in the spirit of debate and to see how well you can organise your ideas, and are not attempts to see if a candidate knows the 'right' answer. You should present all sides of an argument, and not merely the one which you favour. Give a structure to the way you display your knowledge and opinions, and *support what you say with close reference to the text.* Be disciplined: never allow yourself to get away with vague, general statements without referring to an appropriate part of the play in order to substantiate what you say. Quote where necessary – and remember that peppering your essay with single words or short phrases from the play in single quotation marks can be as effective as longer quotations. You should take the initiative and provide a focus when the question is very general: this kind is usually more difficult than one on a specific aspect of the play, and it is easy to lose your way. N.B. The sections in Parts 1 and 3 of these Notes which are essentially background material (for example, *The setting*) are intended to help you to understand the atmosphere of the play. The information therein should be used very sparingly in an essay, and should never be allowed to crowd out a close consideration of the text.

The titles below are in no particular order, any more than the examiner will choose to ask you one particular question rather than another. Having thought about a title, you may wish to follow the procedure set out in note (*e*) of *Preparing for the examination* above.

(1) In what ways is *The Changeling* a play with a moral?

(2) How far are Beatrice and De Flores tragic figures?

(3) Consider the relationship between love and madness in the play.

(4) 'Things are never as they seem.' Show how the play explores the gap between appearance and reality, between the way things seem and the way they are.

(5) What kind of comparison do you think the playwrights intend us to make between Isabella and Beatrice?

(6) What does the subplot contribute to the play?
(7) Is the plot of *The Changeling* well constructed?
(8) 'A colourless character'. Is this a fair view of Alsemero? Assess his role in the play.
(9) What do you consider to be the main themes of the play?
(10) What do (a) Vermandero, (b) Alonzo de Piracquo, and (c) Tomazo de Piracquo contribute to the play?
(11) 'A tragedy of ordinary people, whom we can recognise and with whom we are able to identify and sympathise.' Discuss this view of the play.
(12) Trace the course of the relationship between De Flores and Beatrice.
(13) Apply the following quotation to the play:

> Our eyes are sentinels unto our judgments,
> And should give certain judgment what they see;
> But they are rash sometimes and tell us wonders
> Of common things, which, when our judgments find,
> They then can check the eyes and call them blind.
>
> (I.1.72–6)

(14) 'A play about wilful people who lack self-awareness and deceive themselves'. Consider this view of *The Changeling*.
(15) 'A study in sin and retribution'. Consider this view of the play.
(16) Consider the use of irony in the play.
(17) Why is the play called *The Changeling*? Is there more than one changeling in the play?
(18) Discuss how the imagery of the play contributes to its overall tone and mood.
(19) 'We are not being invited by the playwrights to blame Beatrice, but to observe and pity her.' Discuss.

Some of the questions above overlap, for example, (2) and (11), but this does not matter: they are all good practice. Questions such as (8) and (10) are good exercises, but you will be lucky to be asked for so straightforward an approach in an examination paper. It is much more likely that you will be asked to view a character from a particular angle; and in writing your answer you must make sure that what you write is strictly relevant to the question, and that you do not merely unload all the information you have about a character, or just tell the story.

Specimen answers

Below are specimen answers to questions (7), (9), (16) and (17). If you would like to write an answer yourself to these questions then you should do so before reading the attempts that follow. You will notice that elements from Part 3 of these Notes have been used, where appropriate: but they have been used sparingly, only the strictly relevant pieces being incorporated. Line references are given purely as guides – you would not be expected to remember them exactly (see *In the examination*, note (10), above). It is emphasised that the following four answers are 'attempts'. They are quite good attempts, or they would not be worth printing here: but it must not be taken that they are 'model' or 'correct' answers.

---

(7) Is the plot of *The Changeling* well constructed?

The structure of *The Changeling* is simple and consistent, and the story is told in straightforward but powerful language. The play contains two scenes of exceptional dramatic quality, II.2. and III.4, but, while much of the play draws its power from the context of these two scenes, it would be a mistake to consider that the plot hinges on them, as some critics have done. The play must be seen as a unity, the full meaning of which is not made clear until the final scene. For a collaboration the play is remarkably successful, and if we did not know that it was written by two men it would be unlikely that we would guess it. In fact, it is more or less agreed that Rowley wrote the first and last scenes and the subplot, and Middleton the rest. The construction of the play is so even that it is a fair assumption that the overall plan was the responsibility of one of them.

In the first scene we are introduced to the first transformation of the play, that of Alsemero from a traveller indifferent to women to a lover and gallant. Jasperino's bawdy talk with Diaphanta introduces us to the lust that runs beneath the surface appearance of many of the characters in both plots; at least Jaserpino and Diaphanta are direct about it – there is no hiding in what they are mutually interested (see I.1.137–53). De Flores is introduced, and Beatrice's reaction to him, and we see how the characters' wills are already changing them. When Beatrice says 'I shall change my saint, I fear me; I find/A giddy turning in me' (I.1.156–7), she speaks words that could equally well have come from Alsemero. Vermandero will 'want my will else' if Beatrice is not quickly married to Alonzo, and her defiant reply aside indicates to us that the mixture of self-willed people is ominous, and this is confirmed when De Flores declares in the final line of the scene 'Though I get nothing else, I'll have my will.'

Thus, by the end of the first scene in the play the audience is introduced to a series of major themes and is given an insight into the natures of the principal characters. Act I Scene 2 is the first of three subplot scenes in which we find the concerns of the main plot echoed on a more literal level. The disguising of inner intentions by outward appearance which is manifested to the audience (but not, of course, to the other characters) by frequent asides in the main plot is demonstrated by actual disguise of clothing. Deception and self-deception are seen, as in the main plot; and self-awareness too, that of Tomazo in the main plot (see V.2) being parallelled by Isabella's common sense throughout the subplot. As the play progresses, these themes continue to be echoed and developed in two further subplot scenes, Act III Scene 3 and Act IV Scene 3.

The content of wills reaches its initial climax in Act II Scene 2, where De Flores receives his 'commission' to kill Alonzo. The scene is excellently constructed, with De Flores and Beatrice becoming increasingly excited with the prospect of getting what they want (in both cases their end is lust, although De Flores is the more consciously aware of the fact), until a climax of short, panting sentences:

> DE FLORES: ... the thought ravishes.
> BEATRICE: Then take him to thy fury!
> DE FLORES: I thirst for him.
> BEATRICE: Alonzo de Piracquo!
> DE FLORES: His end's upon him ...
>
> (II.2.132–5)

It is an orgasm, for which death – a concealed metaphor here – was a common Elizabethan euphemism.

The course of action determined upon, the build-up to and the execution of the murder of Alonzo in Act III are swift, and in Act III Scene 4 the pretences are stripped away. De Flores is made to be quite explicit as Beatrice refuses to face the truth of what she is – a murderess, and what she must become – De Flores's whore. The moment she submits to this realisation, De Flores becomes gentle and the scene ends on a quiet note: 'Silence is one of pleasure's best receipts;/Thy peace is wrought for ever in this yielding' (III.4.168–9).

Act IV opens with a dumb-show, with gentlemen seen applauding the choice of Alsemero to replace the missing Alonzo as bridegroom, and with Beatrice entering as a bride. These happy associations, which on the face of it illustrate the achievement of desires, are immediately contrasted with Beatrice's soliloquoy which follows (compare Act III of Shakespeare's *Macbeth*). Beatrice is presumably wearing the full array of a virgin bride as she tells of her deflowering, saying that she has been 'undone ... endlessly' (IV.1.1). She now recognises the reality of her isolation. Some critics consider that the quality of the plot deteriorates from this point; this is arguable, but it cannot be denied that the structure remains tight. The virginity test may have a touch of absurdity about it, but it is a symbol of the traps which now beset Beatrice. Her husband is now 'a cunning gamester' whom she must do her best to outwit, and she shows herself no better judge of character than she did with De Flores when she employs Diaphanta as a substitute for her herself in the bridal bed.

As the play moves into Act V we can see that she is to have no peace. She is a picture of pathetic humilation as she waits in the darkness for Diaphanta to give her back her place in the marriage bed. The ruse of the fire gives her a temporary breathing space, but with the appearance of the ghost before her and the brooding intuition of the potential revenger, Tomazo, in the background but closing in (see IV.2 and V.2), we know that her inevitable discovery cannot be long delayed. It is a weakness of the plot that it is just another reported sighting of a meeting between her and De Flores which precipitates the final confrontation between Alsemero and Beatrice (who again misjudges by thinking that Alsmero will think less of murder than of adultery), and between Alsemero and De Flores. The play gathers to a head quickly, with Beatrice shouting denials from the closet, De Flores's open defiance, and the deaths of the guilty pair, with Beatrice's final recognition, tragic or merely pathetic depending on your viewpoint, that she is morally De Flores's twin and a fit mate for him, and that ' 'Tis time to die when 'tis a shame to live' (V.3.179). Alsemero sums up the moral of it all and helps guide the other characters to a greater awareness, and the play moves quietly to a close.

Overall, the structure of this play is remarkable for its tightness and economy. Within that, some of the richest and most action-packed scenes in the play are comparatively short: for instance, II.2, III.4 and V.1 are all between one and two hundred lines in length.

---

(9) What do you consider to be the main themes of the play?

Depending on the emphasis given in different productions, or on the particular viewpoint of a reader of the play, *The Changeling* can be seen basically to be about different things. It shows how driving self-will leads to the adoption of the ultimate resort of murder in order to clear the way to the desired object. It is a demonstration that love needs to be guided by reason: if so, it can be a force for immeasurable good; if allowed to go out of control it can become mere lust and bring about a catastrophe. The play can be seen as essentially a study in sin and retribution. Middleton does not focus the story upon the reactions of Alsemero, the righteous and betrayed man, as in the main source to the play; the concentration is upon Beatrice's dilemma and the moral retribution that comes upon her. Her first reflective thought, after acting with impetuosity and lack of forethought for three Acts of the play, is when she realises that there is no escaping the consequences of what she has done: 'Vengeance begins;/Murder, I see, is followed by more sins' (III.4.163–4).

One of the main themes in the play is the gap between outward sight and inward reality, between the way things appear and the way they really are. Alsemero is attracted to Beatrice at the beginning of the play by her beauty. His will temporarily overcomes his judgment, and while his will predominates he is deceived as to Beatrice's true nature. Only later, when his reason comes into play and he takes seriously the warnings of his friends, do the sinners need to fear discovery. Alonzo also judges by appearances, but he is not even warned by what is in front of his eyes and what his brother plainly sees. Alonzo's desire to win Beatrice is such that he suffers from 'love's tame madness'. It is ironic that the clearest statement concerning sight/insight is given by Beatrice in the first scene of the play, and is presented as a warning to Alsemero:

> Our eyes are sentinels unto our judgments,
> And should give certain judgment what they see;
> But they are rash sometimes and tell us wonders
> Of common things, which, when our judgments find,
> They then can check the eyes and call them blind.
>
> (I.1.72–6)

In the main plot, judgment by the eyes only leads to deception; in the subplot this idea is made an explicit image by the device of changed clothes forming a disguise which is, by theatrical convention, impenetrable.

The main function of the subplot is to enable the audience to absorb two of the main themes of the play: that appearances are deceptive, and that men and women will willingly become changelings and undergo a transformation when love/lust is at stake. Alsemero changes from a traveller to a lover so swiftly that his friend Jasperino is amazed. Beatrice changes from viewing De Flores with horror to declaring that 'Here's a man worth loving' (V.1.76). She changes Alonzo for Alsemero for De Flores as the object of her desire. Diaphanta takes her place in the bridal bed. The word 'change' is used nineteen times in the play.

The thematic connection between the main plot and the subplot is made clear in the moralising of the final scene:

> ALSEMERO: What an opacous body had that moon
> That last chang'd on us! Here's beauty chang'd
> To ugly whoredom; here, servant obedience
> To a master-sin, imperious murder;
> I, a suppos'd husband, chang'd embraces
> With wantonness, but that was paid before;
> Your change is come too, from an ignorant wrath
> To knowing friendship. Are there any more on's?
>
> ANTONIO: Yes, sir I was chang'd too, from a little ass as I was to a great fool as I am, and had been like to ha' been chang'd to the gallows, but that you know my innocence always excuses me.

FRANCISCUS: I was chang'd from a little wit to be stark mad,
Almost for the same purpose.
ISABELLA: (*to* ALIBIUS): Your change is still behind
But deserve your best transformation. . . .
ALIBIUS: I see all apparent, wife, and will change now
Into a better husband.

(V.3.196–214)

Finally, the expression of attraction and repulsion, usually sexual, is predominantly seen in terms of food and poison in the play, particularly in connection with De Flores. Love for him is an appetite, but he himself, by others, is several times seen as poison, or a poisonous reptile such as a snake.

In this essay above you would not, of course, be able to quote the long extract from Act V. It is reproduced here because it is all relevant to the argument in hand, and you would be expected to be able to refer to its substance in your own words, and perhaps to throw in an occasional word or phrase that will help to give the flavour of the original.

---

(16) Consider the use of irony in the play.

Most , but not all, of the ironies in *The Changeling* are generated through the characters' lack of awareness, rather than by circumstances about which they could not possibly know. In the very first scene Beatrice makes platitudinous remarks to Alsemero about the danger of making rash judgments, blithely oblivious that she should be applying that advice to herself:

Our eyes are sentinels unto our judgments,
And should give certain judgment what they see;
But they are rash and sometimes tell us wonders
Of common things, which, when our judgments find,
They then can check the eyes and call them blind.

(I.1.72–6)

We are all, however, bad at taking our own advice, and we would be rash to hurry to condemn Beatrice here; it is an ironic tragedy that when she gains some awareness at the end of Act III Scene 4 it is too late.

The great scenes of irony in the play which are great in other ways too are II.2 and III.4. In II.2 Beatrice thinks that her persuasive talking has manipulated De Flores into a mood of willing subservience in which he will do anything she wants, and by the end of the scene she is rejoicing secretly that she shall be getting rid 'Of two inveterate loathings at one time,/Piracquo, and his dog-face' (II.2.146–7). We in the audience know that at the very moment she says this she has entered a trap which will soon be sprung (in III.4). Admittedly, De Flores is taken in at first ('Ha, I shall run mad with joy! . . .' – II.2.70), but only fleetingly, and his critical faculties which lead him to question the other person's motivation soon come into play:

'Tis the same physnomy, to a hair and pimple,
Which she called scurvy scarce an hour ago;
How is this? (II.2.76–8)

Immediately he has come to terms with the situation he knows precisely how he will use it. She thinks that all he wants is money, and the scene generates a deal of eroticism from the irony that she thinks that she is exciting him to serve her – which she is, but not in the way she imagines. When she assures him that his 'reward shall be precious' he replies:

That I have thought on;
I have assur'd myself of that beforehand.
And know it will be precious; the thought ravishes.
(II.2.130–2)

He might have said to her, as he says to the equally deceived Alonzo only a few minutes later, 'you shall see anon/A place you little dream on' (III.2.1–2). The audience is alive to all the dramatic ironies while II.2 is actually in progress. The only element which is left slightly ambiguous is whether De Flores is deceived into thinking at any stage that Beatrice is prepared to offer herself as a reward to him; on this point critical opinion varies.

In the next scene between them, III.4, the ironies begin immediately. Beatrice sheds tears at the news of the death of her betrothed, but they are tears of joy, not sorrow. When De Flores offers her the dead man's finger she sees a certain horror of the murder, but fails to see the symbolic sexual suggestiveness of De Flores's gesture. However, by the end of the scene, Beatrice at last understands: there are no ironies left – and no escape either.

During the last two acts of the play the ironies spring mainly from Beatrice's and De Flores's deception of others. Diaphanta asserts her maidenhood, urging the deflowered Beatrice that 'Your honourable self is not a truer' (IV.1.94). Tomazo de Piracquo, remembers that 'My brother lov'd thee well' (IV.2.43) and appeals to 'Honest De Flores' to help him find the murderer, to which De Flores replies, ' 'Las, sir/I am so charitable I think none/Worse than myself' (IV.2.47–9), leading Tomazo to conclude 'That De Flores has a wondrous honest heart' (IV.2.57). Despite his suspicions, Alsemero still only has to look on Beatrice to declare that 'Modesty's shrine is set in yonder forehead' (IV.2.125).

Act V Scene I contains some of the finest touches of irony in the play, and they continue to be made possible by the changed nature of the relationship between Beatrice and De Flores: we see them working ever more closely together, 'twins in mischief'; but the other characters still do not see what we see, and this is the essence of dramatic irony. Diaphanta is sent to her chamber for her 'reward'; Alsemero joins the bride who he thinks has just left his bed, assuming that she is trembling because of her fear of the fire; Vermandero agrees with Beatrice that De Flores is a 'wondrous necessary man' (V.1.91), who enters deploring the death of 'poor virginity' (Diaphanta); Alsemero encourages Beatrice to shed 'Not a tear more;/I charge you by the last embrace I gave you/In bed before this rais'd us' (V.1.109–11); Beatrice prompts her father and husband into agreeing to reward De Flores for his efficiency in dealing with the fire, a 'trick' which calls forth admiration even from the cynical De Flores.

The subplot is a burlesque which provides an ironic comment on the main action of the play throughout. The clear sight of Isabella parallels the blindness of Beatrice, the literal antics of Antonio and Franciscus parallel 'love's tame madness' of Alsemero, Alonzo and De Flores, Alibius's asylum, and the confinement of his wife, mirrors in a distorted fashion the claustrophobia of Vermandero's castle and his attitude towards his daughter. A prime example of the way that the subplot comments ironically on the main plot occurs at the end of Act IV, where we see the dance of the fools and madmen; within a couple of minutes we are to witness the 'dance' into which love/lust has led Beatrice on her wedding night.

The end of the play mirrors the end of Act III. Just as the ironies disappeared when Beatrice came to a realisation of the truth, so they melt away during V.3 when Alsemero and the others are forced to recognise the real nature of things.

You will see that I.1.72–6 is quoted in this essay, as it has been more than once elsewhere in these Notes. When a particular quotation keeps cropping up you can be sure it is one of the keys to the play, and you should learn it.

---

(17) Why is the play called *The Changeling*? Is there more than one changeling in the play?

Antonio is listed in the *Dramatis Personae* as 'the Changeling'. He changes his clothes and pretends to be an idiot in order to gain access to Isabella; and he is doubly a changeling, because it is 'love's tame madness' which has caused him to lose his judgment in his lust for Isabella. However, the full significance of the title is quite lost if it is not appreciated that there are other changelings in the play. Franciscus, Alsemero, Tomazo, De Flores, Diaphanta, Alonzo and Beatrice are all changelings in varying ways and to different degrees. Isabella is the only character who positively resists the temptation to be a changeling and remains constant.

The theme of transformation is established in the very first scene. Alsemero, a hardener traveller who is indifferent to women, is changed by superficial contact with Beatrice into a vacillating lover; the change is so striking that his friend Jasperino comments on it with amazement. Alsemero thinks of himself as constant (I.1.35), but the weather vane seems to symbolise the uncertain state of his mind. Beatrice is the chief changeling in the play; the dictionary lists 'inconstant woman' as a usual meaning of the word 'changeling'. By line 85 of the play she is shown deciding, before she can have had any time to get to know Alsemero, that 'This was the man was meant me'; so she changes from loving Alonzo to loving Alsemero. Later she changes from loving him to loving De Flores and, at the same time, from loathing De Flores to loving him. It is this changeableness, brought on by lust, which triggers the tragedy: the exchange of Alsemero for De Flores leads ultimately to the change of life for death, heaven for hell. The changeling/substitute-in-the-marriage-bed Diaphanta, who is a maid yet lecherously eager to lose that maidenhead, is an explicit manifestation of the real nature of Beatrice which lies under the veneer. Such a readiness to exchange roles costs both of them their lives.

Alsemero, and the characters of the subplot, sum up at the end of the play the changes which have occurred. Alsemero hints at the influence of the changeable moon (V.3.196–7 – and see also III.3.82–90), which affects the sound judgments of people, turning them into fools and lunatics. Beatrice is 'beauty chang'd/To ugly whoredom': De Flores shows a change from 'servant obedience/To master-sin, imperious murder'; he himself 'a suppos'd husband' who 'chang'd embraces/With wantonness' (Diaphanta); turning to Tomazo, he says that 'Your change is come too, from an ignorant wrath/To knowing friendship'; and then he asks whether there are any other changelings present. Antonio immediately responds that he 'was chang'd too, from a little ass as I was to a great fool as I am, and had been like to ha' been changed to the gallows'; Franciscus chimes in that he 'was chang'd from a little wit to be stark mad,/Almost for the same purpose.' Isabella points out to her husband, Alibius, that he too must learn from his mistakes and change, and he replies that now he sees clearly and 'will change now/Into a better husband.'

The word 'change' appears nineteen times in the play, and its variant forms many times more. The rather matter-of-fact ending, where the characters 'see all apparent', holds out the prospect that the kind of constancy to which Isabella has clung will prevail, and that fickle changeableness is exposed for what it is.

In the penultimate paragraph of this answer, the same section of the play (V.3.196–214) has been discussed as was quoted in full in the specimen answer to question (9) above. However, on this occasion the quotation has been broken down and used sensibly in the way that was suggested in the footnote at the end of the answer to question (9).

Context questions

A context question is one where a passage from the play is reproduced in the question paper, and you are asked one or more questions on that passage. If you are set one of these, remember that you must concentrate on the passage set, and may only discuss matters concerning the play as a whole if the question invites you to do so. An example of a context question might be as follows: II.2.57–98 ('I have watched this meeting . . . Oh, my De Flores!') is printed out in full. The questions that follow ask you (i) What is the exact context of the passage? (ii) In what ways are themes and character traits touched on in this passage central to the play? You may also be asked to explain briefly the meanings of certain words and phrases in the play; for this, as for (i) above, there is no substitute for knowing the play thoroughly. (ii) must be answered with close reference to the passage, although it will be accepted that the characters of Beatrice and De Flores and significant issues in the play will have to be mentioned briefly in general terms in order for you to show what is happening in the passage set.

Part 5

Suggestions for further reading

The text

The following editions of *The Changeling* are available:

The Revels edition, ed. N.W. Bawcutt, Methuen, London, 1958. This has a very full introductory essay and is the most scholarly edition of the play.

The Mathew Carey Library edition, ed. Matthew W. Black, University of Pennsylvania Press, Philadelphia, 1966. This has some lively footnotes, although the interpretation of some of the words is suspect.

The Plays by Renaissance and Restoration Dramatists series includes *The Changeling* in a volume of *The Selected Plays of Thomas Middleton*, ed. David L. Frost, Cambridge University Press, Cambridge, 1978. The text is printed in a clear type-face and there are good, uncomplicated footnotes. This edition is highly recommended, and all line references in these Notes are taken from it.

The New Mermaid edition, ed. Patricia Thomson, Benn, London, 1964. This contains quite a good introductory essay, but the footnotes are minimal and the edition is not recommended for a newcomer to the play.

The Regents Renaissance Drama edition, ed. George Walton Williams, Edward Arnold, London, 1966. This contains quite a good introductory essay and adequate notes.

Critical works on *The Changeling*

It does not matter if you cannot obtain any of the books below. It is your reactions to the play that matter. In any event, get to know the play well first; only then will these critical works offer insights.

BARKER, R.H.: *Thomas Middleton*, Columbia University Press, New York, 1958, pp. 121–31.

BROOKE, NICHOLAS: *Horrid Laughter in Jacobean Tragedy*, Open Books, London, 1979, pp. 70–88.

ENGLEBERG, E.: 'Tragic Blindness in *The Changeling* and *Women Beware Women*', *Modern Language Quarterly*, 23 (1962), pp. 20–28.

FARR, DOROTHY M.: *Thomas Middleton and the Drama of Realism*, Oliver and Boyd, Edinburgh, 1973, Chapter 4, pp. 50–71.

RICKS, CHRISTOPHER: 'The Moral and Poetical Structure of *The Changeling*', *Essays in Criticism*, July 1960, pp. 290–306.

Background reading

BENTLEY, G. E.: *The Jacobean and Caroline Stage*, Clarendon Press, Oxford, 1941–56.

BOWERS, F. T.: *Elizabethan Revenge Tragedy, 1587*–1642, Princeton University Press, Princeton, 1940.

BRADBROOK, M. C.: *Themes and Conventions of Elizabethan Tragedy*, Cambridge University Press, Cambridge, 1935.

BRITTIN, N. A.: *Thomas Middleton* (Twayne's English Author series), Twayne, New York, 1972.

CUNNINGHAM, JOHN E.: *Elizabethan and Early Stuart Drama* (Literature in Perspective series), Evans, London, 1965.

ELIOT, T. S.: 'Thomas Middleton', reprinted in *Elizabethan Dramatists*, Faber, London, 1963, pp. 83–106.

ELLIS-FERMOR, UNA: *The Jacobean Drama*, Methuen, London, 1936.

EMPSON, WILLIAM: *Some Versions of Pastoral*, Chatto and Windus, London, 1935.

GARDNER, HELEN: 'The Tragedy of Damnation' in *Elizabethan Drama*, ed. R. Kauffman, Oxford University Press, New York, 1961.

HIBBARD, G. R.: 'The Tragedies of Thomas Middleton and the Decadence of the Drama', *University of Nottingham Renaissance and Modern Studies*, I, 1957.

HOLMES, D. H.: *The Art of Thomas Middleton: a Critical Study*, Clarendon Press, Oxford, 1970.

KNIGHTS, L. C.: *Drama and Society in the Age of Jonson*, Chatto and Windus, London, 1937.

POTTER, LOIS (ED.): *The Revels History of Drama in English, Volume IV, 1613*–60, Methuen, London, 1981.

RIBNER, IRVING: *Jacobean Tragedy*, Methuen, London, 1962.

SCHOENBAUM, SAMUEL: *Middleton's Tragedies*, Columbia University Press, New York, 1955.

TOMLINSON, T. B.: *A Study of Elizabethan and Jacobean Tragedy*, Oxford University Press, Oxford, 1964.

The author of these notes

Neil King was educated at Sherborne School, and the Universities of Durham and Cambridge. He has taught in schools in Stockton-on-Tees, Watford, Bushey and Cambridge and has been an examiner in English Literature for five different examination boards. At present he is Senior Master and Head of English at Hymers College, Hull, and is engaged on research into aspects of moral and dramatic tension in Elizabethan and Jacobean Revenge Tragedy. He has compiled a drama series for schools which covers all aspects of the theatre from the Greeks to the twentieth century, has edited *She Stoops to Conquer* and *Romeo and Juliet* for Longman, and is the author of York Notes on *Everyman, The Duchess of Malfi, The Revenger's Tragedy, The Changeling* and *The Relapse,* and has written and co-authored plays which have been performed at Durham, Hull, Cambridge and the Edinburgh Festival. He was appointed Schoolmaster Fellow of Fitzwilliam College, Cambridge, in 1982.

York Notes: list of titles

CHINUA ACHEBE
A Man of the People
Arrow of God
Things Fall Apart

EDWARD ALBEE
Who's Afraid of Virginia Woolf?

ELECHI AMADI
The Concubine

ANONYMOUS
Beowulf
Everyman

JOHN ARDEN
Serjeant Musgrave's Dance

AYI KWEI ARMAH
The Beautyful Ones Are Not Yet Born

W. H. AUDEN
Selected Poems

JANE AUSTEN
Emma
Mansfield Park
Northanger Abbey
Persuasion
Pride and Prejudice
Sense and Sensibility

HONORÉ DE BALZAC
Le Père Goriot

SAMUEL BECKETT
Waiting for Godot

SAUL BELLOW
Henderson, The Rain King

ARNOLD BENNETT
Anna of the Five Towns

WILLIAM BLAKE
Songs of Innocence, Songs of Experience

ROBERT BOLT
A Man For All Seasons

ANNE BRONTË
The Tenant of Wildfell Hall

CHARLOTTE BRONTË
Jane Eyre

EMILY BRONTË
Wuthering Heights

ROBERT BROWNING
Men and Women

JOHN BUCHAN
The Thirty-Nine Steps

JOHN BUNYAN
The Pilgrim's Progress

BYRON
Selected Poems

ALBERT CAMUS
L'Etranger (The Outsider)

GEOFFREY CHAUCER
Prologue to the Canterbury Tales
The Franklin's Tale
The Knight's Tale
The Merchant's Tale
The Miller's Tale
The Nun's Priest's Tale
The Pardoner's Tale
The Wife of Bath's Tale
Troilus and Criseyde

ANTON CHEKHOV
The Cherry Orchard

SAMUEL TAYLOR COLERIDGE
Selected Poems

WILKIE COLLINS
The Moonstone
The Woman in White

SIR ARTHUR CONAN DOYLE
The Hound of the Baskervilles

WILLIAM CONGREVE
The Way of the World

JOSEPH CONRAD
Heart of Darkness
Lord Jim
Nostromo
The Secret Agent
Victory
Youth and *Typhoon*

STEPHEN CRANE
The Red Badge of Courage

BRUCE DAWE
Selected Poems

WALTER DE LA MARE
Selected Poems

DANIEL DEFOE
A Journal of the Plague Year
Moll Flanders
Robinson Crusoe

CHARLES DICKENS
A Tale of Two Cities
Bleak House
David Copperfield
Great Expectations
Hard Times
Little Dorrit
Nicholas Nickleby
Oliver Twist
Our Mutual Friend
The Pickwick Papers

EMILY DICKINSON
Selected Poems

JOHN DONNE
Selected Poems

THEODORE DREISER
Sister Carrie

GEORGE ELIOT
Adam Bede
Middlemarch
Silas Marner
The Mill on the Floss

T. S. ELIOT
Four Quartets
Murder in the Cathedral
Selected Poems
The Cocktail Party
The Waste Land

J. G. FARRELL
The Siege of Krishnapur

GEORGE FARQUHAR
The Beaux Stratagem

WILLIAM FAULKNER
Absalom, Absalom!
As I Lay Dying
Go Down, Moses
The Sound and the Fury

HENRY FIELDING
Joseph Andrews
Tom Jones

F. SCOTT FITZGERALD
Tender is the Night
The Great Gatsby

E. M. FORSTER
A Passage to India
Howards End

ATHOL FUGARD
Selected Plays

JOHN GALSWORTHY
Strife

MRS GASKELL
North and South

WILLIAM GOLDING
Lord of the Flies
The Inheritors
The Spire

OLIVER GOLDSMITH
She Stoops to Conquer
The Vicar of Wakefield

ROBERT GRAVES
Goodbye to All That

GRAHAM GREENE
Brighton Rock
The Heart of the Matter
The Power and the Glory

THOMAS HARDY
Far from the Madding Crowd
Jude the Obscure
Selected Poems
Tess of the D'Urbervilles
The Mayor of Casterbridge
The Return of the Native
The Trumpet Major
The Woodlanders
Under the Greenwood Tree

L. P. HARTLEY
The Go-Between
The Shrimp and the Anemone

NATHANIEL HAWTHORNE
The Scarlet Letter

SEAMUS HEANEY
Selected Poems

ERNEST HEMINGWAY
A Farewell to Arms
For Whom the Bell Tolls
The African Stories
The Old Man and the Sea

GEORGE HERBERT
Selected Poems

HERMANN HESSE
Steppenwolf

BARRY HINES
Kes

HOMER
The Iliad

ANTHONY HOPE
The Prisoner of Zenda

GERARD MANLEY HOPKINS
Selected Poems

WILLIAM DEAN HOWELLS
The Rise of Silas Lapham

RICHARD HUGHES
A High Wind in Jamaica

THOMAS HUGHES
Tom Brown's Schooldays

ALDOUS HUXLEY
Brave New World

HENRIK IBSEN
A Doll's House
Ghosts
Hedda Gabler

HENRY JAMES
Daisy Miller
The Europeans
The Portrait of a Lady
The Turn of the Screw
Washington Square

SAMUEL JOHNSON
Rasselas

BEN JONSON
The Alchemist
Volpone

JAMES JOYCE
A Portrait of the Artist as a Young Man
Dubliners

JOHN KEATS
Selected Poems

RUDYARD KIPLING
Kim

D. H. LAWRENCE
Sons and Lovers
The Rainbow
Women in Love

CAMARA LAYE
L'Enfant Noir

HARPER LEE
To Kill a Mocking-Bird

LAURIE LEE
Cider with Rosie

THOMAS MANN
Tonio Kröger

CHRISTOPHER MARLOWE
Doctor Faustus
Edward II

ANDREW MARVELL
Selected Poems

W. SOMERSET MAUGHAM
Of Human Bondage
Selected Short Stories

J. MEADE FALKNER
Moonfleet

HERMAN MELVILLE
Billy Budd
Moby Dick

THOMAS MIDDLETON
Women Beware Women

THOMAS MIDDLETON *and* WILLIAM ROWLEY
The Changeling

ARTHUR MILLER
Death of a Salesman
The Crucible

JOHN MILTON
Paradise Lost I & II
Paradise Lost IV & IX
Selected Poems

V. S. NAIPAUL
A House for Mr Biswas

SEAN O'CASEY
Juno and the Paycock
The Shadow of a Gunman

GABRIEL OKARA
The Voice

EUGENE O'NEILL
Mourning Becomes Electra

GEORGE ORWELL
Animal Farm
Nineteen Eighty-four

JOHN OSBORNE
Look Back in Anger

WILFRED OWEN
Selected Poems

ALAN PATON
Cry, The Beloved Country

THOMAS LOVE PEACOCK
Nightmare Abbey and *Crotchet Castle*

HAROLD PINTER
The Birthday Party
The Caretaker

PLATO
The Republic

ALEXANDER POPE
Selected Poems

THOMAS PYNCHON
The Crying of Lot 49

SIR WALTER SCOTT
Ivanhoe
Quentin Durward
The Heart of Midlothian
Waverley

PETER SHAFFER
The Royal Hunt of the Sun

WILLIAM SHAKESPEARE
A Midsummer Night's Dream
Antony and Cleopatra
As You Like It
Coriolanus
Cymbeline
Hamlet
Henry IV Part I
Henry IV Part II
Henry V
Julius Caesar
King Lear
Love's Labour's Lost
Macbeth
Measure for Measure
Much Ado About Nothing
Othello
Richard II
Richard III
Romeo and Juliet
Sonnets
The Merchant of Venice
The Taming of the Shrew
The Tempest
The Winter's Tale
Troilus and Cressida
Twelfth Night
The Two Gentlemen of Verona

GEORGE BERNARD SHAW
Androcles and the Lion
Arms and the Man
Caesar and Cleopatra
Candida
Major Barbara
Pygmalion
Saint Joan
The Devil's Disciple

MARY SHELLEY
Frankenstein

PERCY BYSSHE SHELLEY
Selected Poems

RICHARD BRINSLEY SHERIDAN
The School for Scandal
The Rivals

WOLE SOYINKA
The Lion and the Jewel
The Road
Three Short Plays

EDMUND SPENSER
The Faerie Queene (Book I)

JOHN STEINBECK
Of Mice and Men
The Grapes of Wrath
The Pearl

LAURENCE STERNE
A Sentimental Journey
Tristram Shandy

ROBERT LOUIS STEVENSON
Kidnapped
Treasure Island
Dr Jekyll and Mr Hyde

TOM STOPPARD
Professional Foul
Rosencrantz and Guildenstern are Dead

JONATHAN SWIFT
Gulliver's Travels

JOHN MILLINGTON SYNGE
The Playboy of the Western World

TENNYSON
Selected Poems

W. M. THACKERAY
Vanity Fair

DYLAN THOMAS
Under Milk Wood

EDWARD THOMAS
Selected Poems

FLORA THOMPSON
Lark Rise to Candleford

J. R. R. TOLKIEN
The Hobbit
The Lord of the Rings

CYRIL TOURNEUR
The Revenger's Tragedy

ANTHONY TROLLOPE
Barchester Towers

MARK TWAIN
Huckleberry Finn
Tom Sawyer

VIRGIL
The Aeneid

VOLTAIRE
Candide

EVELYN WAUGH
Decline and Fall
A Handful of Dust

JOHN WEBSTER
The Duchess of Malfi
The White Devil

H. G. WELLS
The History of Mr Polly
The Invisible Man
The War of the Worlds

ARNOLD WESKER
Chips with Everything
Roots

PATRICK WHITE
Voss

OSCAR WILDE
The Importance of Being Earnest

TENNESSEE WILLIAMS
The Glass Menagerie

VIRGINIA WOOLF
To the Lighthouse

WILLIAM WORDSWORTH
Selected Poems

W. B. YEATS
Selected Poems

York Handbooks: list of titles

YORK HANDBOOKS form a companion series to York Notes and are designed to meet the wider needs of students of English and related fields. Each volume is a compact study of a given subject area, written by an authority with experience in communicating the essential ideas to students of all levels.

AN INTRODUCTORY GUIDE TO ENGLISH LITERATURE
by MARTIN STEPHEN

PREPARING FOR EXAMINATIONS IN ENGLISH LITERATURE
by NEIL McEWAN

EFFECTIVE STUDYING
by STEVE ROBERTSON *and* DAVID SMITH

THE ENGLISH NOVEL
by IAN MILLIGAN

ENGLISH POETRY
by CLIVE T. PROBYN

STUDYING CHAUCER
by ELISABETH BREWER

STUDYING SHAKESPEARE
by MARTIN STEPHEN *and* PHILIP FRANKS

AN A·B·C OF SHAKESPEARE
by P. C. BAYLEY

STUDYING MILTON
by GEOFFREY M. RIDDEN

STUDYING CHARLES DICKENS
by K. J. FIELDING

STUDYING THOMAS HARDY
by LANCE ST JOHN BUTLER

ENGLISH LITERATURE FROM THE THIRD WORLD
by TREVOR JAMES

ENGLISH USAGE
by COLIN G. HEY

ENGLISH GRAMMAR
by LORETO TODD

STYLE IN ENGLISH PROSE
by NEIL McEWAN

AN INTRODUCTION TO LITERARY CRITICISM
by RICHARD DUTTON

A DICTIONARY OF LITERARY TERMS
by MARTIN GRAY

READING THE SCREEN
An Introduction to Film Studies
by JOHN IZOD